Theoretical Approaches in Psychology

Psychology is often considered to be a science. However, it is unique amongst the sciences as it is not governed by a single set of principles or beliefs. Instead, psychologists can draw upon a range of alternative approaches, each of which views the person and the study of the person in very different ways. *Theoretical Approaches in Psychology* introduces and outlines the six main approaches and considers how each has helped psychologists understand human behaviour, thought and feeling.

Matt Jarvis is Senior Teaching Psychologist at Totton College of Further and Higher Education. His previous publications include *Sport Psychology*, also in this series.

Routledge Modular Psychology

Series editors: Cara Flanagan is an A-Level examining board Reviser, and Lecturer at Inverness College. Philip Banyard is Associate Senior Lecturer in Psychology at Nottingham Trent University and the Chief Examiner for OCR A-Level Psychology.

The *Routledge Modular Psychology* series is a completely new approach to introductory level psychology, and especially suitable for students studying AS and A-Level Psychology. Each short book covers a topic in more detail than any large textbook can, allowing teacher and student to select material exactly to suit any particular course or project.

The books have been written especially for those students new to higher-level study, whether at school, college or university. They include specially designed features to help with technique, such as a model essay at an average level with an examiner's comments to show how extra marks can be gained. The authors are all examiners and teachers at the introductory level.

The *Routledge Modular Psychology* texts are all user-friendly and accessible and include the following features:

- sample essays with specialist commentary to show how to achieve a higher grade
- chapter summaries to assist with revision
- progress and review exercises
- glossary of key terms
- summaries of key research
- further reading to stimulate ongoing study and research
- cross-referencing to other books in the series

Also available in this series (titles listed by syllabus section):

ATYPICAL DEVELOPMENT AND ABNORMAL BEHAVIOUR

Psychopathology
John D. Stirling and Jonathan S.E. Hellewell

Therapeutic Approaches in Psychology
Susan Cave

BIO-PSYCHOLOGY

Cortical Functions
John Stirling

The Physiological Basis of Behaviour: Neural and hormonal processes
Kevin Silber

Awareness: Biorhythms, Sleep and Dreaming
Evie Bentley

COGNITIVE PSYCHOLOGY

Memory and Forgetting
John Henderson

Perception: Theory, development and organisation
Paul Rookes and Jane Willson

DEVELOPMENTAL PSYCHOLOGY

Early Socialisation: Sociability and attachment
Cara Flanagan

PERSPECTIVES AND RESEARCH

Controversies in Psychology
Philip Banyard

Ethical Issues in Psychology
Mike Cardwell (forthcoming)

Introducing Research and Data in Psychology: A guide to methods and analysis
Ann Searle

SOCIAL PSYCHOLOGY

Social Influences
Kevin Wren

Interpersonal Relationships
Diana Dwyer

Social Cognition
Donald Pennington (forthcoming)

OTHER TITLES

Sport Psychology
Matt Jarvis

Health Psychology
Anthony Curtis

Psychology and Work
Christine Hodson (forthcoming)

STUDY GUIDE

Exam Success in AEB Psychology
Paul Humphreys

Theoretical Approaches in Psychology

Matt Jarvis

London and Philadelphia

First published 2000
by Routledge
11 New Fetter Lane, London EC4P 4EE

Simultaneously published in the US by Taylor & Francis, Inc.
325 Chestnut Street, Philadelphia, PA 19106

Routledge is an imprint of the Taylor & Francis Group

© 2000 Matt Jarvis

Typeset in Times and Frutiger by Keystroke,
Jacaranda Lodge, Wolverhampton
Printed and bound in Great Britain by
TJ International Ltd, Padstow, Cornwall

British Library Cataloguing in Publication Data
A catalogue record for this book is available from the British Library

Library of Congress Cataloging in Publication Data
Jarvis, Matt, 1966–
    Theoretical approaches in psychology / Matt Jarvis.
        p. cm. — (Approaches and research. Modular psychology)
    Includes bibliographical references (p.) and index.
    ISBN 0–415–19108–4 (pb) — ISBN 0–415–19107–6 (hb)
    1. Psychology. I. Title. II. Series.
    BF121 .J37 2000
    150—dc21   00-028439

ISBN 0–415–19107–6 (hbk)
ISBN 0–415–19108–4 (pbk)

Contents

Illustrations

Figures

Table

Acknowledgements

The series editors and Routledge acknowledge the expert help of Paul Humphreys, Examiner and Reviser for A-Level psychology, in compiling the Study Aids chapter of each book in the series.

They also acknowledge the Associated Examining Board (AEB) for granting permission to use their examination material. The AEB do not accept responsibility for the answers or examiner comment in the Study Aids chapter of this book or any other book in the series.

Introduction

Introduction: one psychology or many?

A popular definition of psychology would be 'the science of mind and behaviour' (Gross, 1996). Although more often than not psychology is considered to be a science, it is unique amongst the sciences in that it is not governed by a single set of principles and beliefs. Instead, psychologists can draw upon a range of alternative approaches, each of which views the person and the study of the person in very different ways. We shall return to the issue of whether psychology is, or should be, a science later in this chapter. The aim of this book is to outline each of the major theoretical approaches or **paradigms** in psychology, and to consider how psychology has helped us understand human behaviour, thoughts and feelings.

As you consider each approach to psychology, it is almost inevitable that you will be drawn to some approaches, whilst others will appeal to you less, and may even seem pointless or illogical. A central principle of this book is that each of the major approaches to psychology has survived because it has something unique to offer us. Rather than speaking of *strengths* and *weaknesses* of each paradigm, it is perhaps more productive to look at what it has contributed to our understanding of human mind and behaviour, and what this approach is unlikely to achieve on its own. We will thus speak of the *contributions* and *limitations* of each approach.

Just as you will probably like some approaches to psychology better than others, so do professional psychologists. Some practising psychologists work strictly within a particular paradigm – we thus have behavioural psychologists, psychodynamic psychologists and humanistic psychologists. However, many psychologists prefer to draw from several approaches, and are said to be *eclectic* in their approach. Academic research in psychology is currently dominated by a cognitive approach (see Chapters 4 and 5). When reading the following case examples you need to remember that most research-oriented cognitive psychologists are not actually concerned with this type of real-life event.

We can apply six broad theoretical approaches to psychology: the behavioural approach, the psychodynamic approach, the humanistic approach, the cognitive approach (including the cognitive-developmental approach), the social approach and the biological approach. Each of these major approaches can be subdivided into more specialist approaches. For example the 'biological approach' actually includes areas of study as diverse as the physiology of the brain, the influences of evolution on human behaviour and the influence of genes on people's individual characteristics. A good way to gain an under-standing of the aims and assumptions of each psychological paradigm is to consider some vignettes and look at how each approach might explain what is happening.

Case examples and explanations

The three following case examples are based on common real-life scenarios, each of which psychologists might be called upon to explain. We can look at what psychologists might make of these situations, based on each of the main theoretical approaches, and see what we might pick from these explanations about the general aims and assumptions of each approach.

Case example 1: Marjorie

Marjorie is a 32-year-old woman, now happily married after an unhappy childhood in which her mother committed suicide when Marjorie was eight. After this Marjorie was brought up by a rather cold and austere aunt. She does not work and has one 8-year-old daughter. Marjorie's husband is a successful banker and the family are well-off, but he works long hours and sees less of his family than they would like. Recently, Marjorie has been feeling depressed. In order to try to cheer herself up, she has been secretly drinking and indulging in shopping sprees.

Explanations

Psychologists might explain Marjorie's feelings and behaviour in quite different ways according to what theoretical approach they chose to adopt. A psychologist adopting a behavioural approach might, for example, suggest that Marjorie failed to get into the habit of *rewarding herself* and enjoying life when living with her austere aunt, and that this pattern of behaviour has persisted into adulthood. Marjorie's current behaviour of drinking and having shopping sprees could be seen from a behavioural perspective as failed attempts to provide herself with rewards in order to try to enjoy life more.

A psychologist adopting a *psychodynamic* viewpoint would probably look at Marjorie's case rather differently. They might be particularly interested in the death of Marjorie's mother, and the fact that her aunt provided little comfort or support during her childhood. From a psychodynamic perspective, Marjorie's depression might be related directly to not being helped to grieve and to the poor quality substitute parenting provided by her aunt.

A psychologist approaching the case from a *humanistic* perspective would probably be interested in all aspects of Marjorie's life, past and present. Because of her unhappy childhood and her isolation as a housewife in adulthood, Marjorie has never had the opportunities to develop a healthy self-image and so failed to grow into the person she could be. She is thus currently *unfulfilled*. From a humanistic perspective Marjorie's depression might be seen as a result of this lack of personal fulfilment.

From a *biological* perspective, given Marjorie's current feelings and behaviour, the current physiology of her brain is probably disrupted. For example, levels of certain *neurotransmitters*, the brain's chemical messengers, are probably lower than in most people. Seen from a biological point of view, this abnormal brain chemistry may be the root cause of Marjorie's condition, or at least a factor in producing her symptoms. The biological psychologist might be particularly interested in the fact that Marjorie's mother committed suicide. This could indicate that depression has been passed on genetically from her mother.

A psychologist looking at Marjorie's case from a *cognitive* standpoint would be particularly interested in what Marjorie was *thinking*, as well as what she was feeling and how she was behaving. It might be for example that Marjorie holds unrealistic and negative beliefs about herself, her situation or her future. If Marjorie sees herself as a failure or a worthless person, or if she sees her life as empty and her future as hopeless, these unhealthy patterns of thinking might be sufficient to result in depression.

Social perspectives look at the position of the individual in relation to both other individuals and society as a whole. From a social perspective, Marjorie might be seen as *disempowered* by a male-dominated society in which she is forced to remain at home, unfulfilled, whilst her husband pursues a satisfying career. Because of the passive way in which society expects women to show their feelings, Marjorie's dissatisfaction would be expected to manifest itself as depression rather than anger or rebellion.

Case example 2: Mark

Mark has recently begun jogging in his forties and discovered that he has a talent for it. He is about to enter the London Marathon and, despite having never been interested in sport until recently, is tipped to do very well. As the day approaches, Mark trains harder and harder, spending most of his free time running. The only thing stopping Mark being completely happy is that he is mourning for his best friend who recently died suddenly from a heart attack.

Explanations

From a *behavioural* perspective, the more Mark trains the better he gets at running. He can see this in the faster times he is achieving and in the fact that he is becoming less tired after each run. Mark is also receiving many admiring comments from his workmates. He has lost weight and believes he is becoming much more attractive to women. All these factors are rewarding or *reinforcing* Mark's running and encouraging him to continue.

A psychologist adopting a *psychodynamic* approach might instead focus attention on the fact that Mark's friend has recently died, and wonder whether Mark's new healthy behaviour is a response (of which he is not thinking because it would be painful to do so) to his fear that he too might die young. A psychodynamic approach would also consider the possible significance of the *nature* of the health-enhancing strategy Mark has chosen. Mark's running could be interpreted as his symbolically running away from his own mortality.

From a *humanistic* perspective, Mark has discovered in his talent for running a way in which he can fulfil his potential as a person. The fact that he is beginning to do this is gaining him positive regard from others, which boosts his self-esteem. With this new-found self-esteem Mark is further inspired to continue trying to achieve all he can as a runner.

From a *biological* perspective, Mark's behaviour could be interpreted in physiological terms. Whenever Mark runs his brain produces chemicals called endorphins, which are chemically quite similar to drugs like heroin. This gives him a 'runner's high'. One reason Mark is running more and more is to enjoy his fix of endorphins!

A psychologist adopting a *cognitive* approach might differ from the others in crediting Mark with making a logical decision to improve his fitness following the realisation that he is now at an age when not keeping fit is seriously endangering his health. A social approach might emphasise Mark's new social identity as an athlete and the fact that we all see some types of social identity – such as that of an athlete – in a positive light and other identities less positively.

Case example 3: Neil and Sandy

Neil has just returned from the pub, where he has been drinking heavily all evening. His wife, Sandy, challenges him about why he did not call to say that he would not be home for dinner. Neil loses control and slaps Sandy. This is not the first time Neil has hit Sandy. Both Neil and Sandy came from violent families and both suffered and witnessed violence as children. Sandy's previous husband would also hit her.

Explanations

A *behavioural* psychologist would probably see Neil's behaviour primarily as the result of imitation of the adult behaviour he witnessed as a child. A behaviourist might also suspect that Neil may have experimented with violent behaviour as a child and received *rewards* in the form of getting his own way.

From a *psychodynamic* perspective, it is highly significant that both Neil and Sandy, who had both come from violent families, ended up in a violent relationship themselves. However, rather than explaining this in terms of learnt behaviour, the psychodynamic psychologist would be more likely to look at the *dynamic* between the couple, in which both were attracted to the other, perhaps because each reminded the other of members of their own family.

From a *humanistic* viewpoint, both Sandy and Neil have both probably received inadequate love, which has left them with poor psychological health. This means that Sandy probably has poor self-esteem, and she might well believe that she does not deserve better treatment than that she gets from Neil. From a humanistic perspective, an important factor in Neil's violent behaviour may be that he has not developed the same capacity most of us have for *empathy* – i.e. being able to perceive and appreciate the feelings of others.

Various *biological* perspectives could be used to explain Neil's behaviour. From a physiological perspective, Neil's behaviour is accompanied by high levels of certain hormones such as adrenaline, and by considerable activity in certain areas of the brain. A biologist might believe that levels of aggression are partially under genetic control and suggest that this might be why aggression appears to run in Neil's family.

From a *cognitive* perspective, what is particularly significant is what Neil and Sandy might be thinking during their exchange. In particular, a psychologist influenced by cognitive psychology would probably wish to know what Neil was thinking when he lost control and hit Sandy. It may be for example that Neil was having irrational and extreme thoughts such as 'I can't stand this any more' or 'she's just trying to wind me up'. In cognitive theory, irrational behaviour is a direct result of this type of illogical thinking.

From a *social* perspective, male violence towards women symbolises and helps maintain the current status quo of a male-dominated society in which women are disempowered. Feminist social psychologists might emphasise that, although violence *as such* towards women is not committed by most men, more subtle abuses are constantly perpetrated by men against women. Some feminist psychologists might also suggest that *all* men benefit from male–female violence because it keeps women in a submissive role and lowers the baseline of what is acceptable male behaviour towards women.

The major features of each psychological approach

Looking at the perspectives that we can bring to bear on these three vignettes, what can we tease out about each major psychological approach? In all these examples the behaviourist approach focuses, as its name suggests, on the *behaviour* of the people. In each case, the behavioural approach seeks to explain behaviour as being *learnt*, for example by imitating others or by repeating behaviour that brought about a reward.

The psychodynamic and humanistic approaches, by contrast, are more concerned with the *emotional* aspects of people's lives rather than their behaviour. The psychodynamic approach places a great deal of importance on childhood experience, particularly parenting, and on motives for our behaviour of which we are not aware. The humanistic approach places more emphasis on the importance of our self-image, and how this is affected by the ways others treat us.

The biological approach focuses less on behaviour or emotion than on the *physiological processes* that underlie them. Biologically based psychologists also tend to emphasise the *genetic* basis of behaviour as opposed to how behaviour can be acquired through experience. Some psychologists are also interested in whether we might have *evolved* certain behaviours because they benefit us in some way.

The cognitive approach has a different emphasis again, seeing *mental processes* as of primary importance. From a cognitive perspective, we can look at the decisions made by Marjorie, Mark, Neil and Sandy in terms of their perception of events, their reasoning about the nature of these events and their decision (which may be logical or otherwise) on how to respond.

Social perspectives stand alone in seeking to emphasise not just how emotion, behaviour and thought appear in the individual, but also how they are affected in all of us by the influence of other people. Social perspectives are also unique in psychology in being unashamedly political, looking for injustice in gender and class relationships.

Scientific and less scientific approaches

Whether psychology is or should be a science is a thorny question and one that refuses to go away or provoke less bitter disputes as psychology matures as a subject. At the end of the nineteenth century, psychology emerged from two very different roots: biology and philosophy. Biology brought a firm scientific base to psychology, and most psychologists have always considered themselves to be scientists and attempted to study psychology in a scientific manner. However not all psychologists agree that adopting the methods of science is really appropriate for studying humans.

We can broadly divide our six psychological approaches down the middle as regards their attitudes to psychology-as-science. Behaviourism, biopsychology and cognitive psychology all favour the scientific approach and see psychology as a hard science. Followers of psychodynamic, humanistic and social approaches are more likely to take a broader view of psychology and not see themselves as bound by science, although they may still conduct scientific research. Indeed, humanistic psychologists tend to reject completely the idea that human nature can be studied scientifically.

Progress exercise

Draw up as many advantages and disadvantages as you can come up with for psychology being a pure science.

Summary

There are six broad theoretical approaches to psychology, each of which focuses on different aspects of psychological phenomena, such as behaviour, emotion and thinking. Each emphasises different influences on the person, for example parenting, genetics and learning. Some approaches are very scientific, others less so.

If you are going to get a fair idea of what real-life psychology is like from reading this book, you should keep in mind the following points concerning the relationship between different approaches and the people that work with them.

- *Some* ideas from all of the main theoretical approaches are widely accepted in psychology. Thus it is not only behaviourists that believe in reinforcement; not only psychodynamic psychologists that believe in the importance of parenting; and not only biologists that accept the importance of genetics.
- Some paradigms are most popular *outside* psychology. Thus, humanistic psychology is most popular in the field of counselling, and psychodynamic approaches tend to be favoured by psychiatrists and social workers rather than by psychologists.
- Some psychologists are eclectic and borrow freely from different approaches whilst others work purely with one approach.

You should now have some idea of where each of the main approaches to psychology is coming from. In the following chapters we shall explore each approach in turn, outlining some major theories and applications, looking in detail at some classic studies, examining a topical issue and evaluating the contributions and limitations of the approach.

Before going on to read the remaining chapters of this book, reflect on your first reactions to each of the major psychological approaches you have just encountered. What has intuitive appeal to you and what (if anything) strikes you as boring, pointless or silly?

Review exercise

Further reading

Lundin, R.W. (1996) *Theories and Systems of Psychology*, Lexington: Heath. A well-detailed and highly academic guide to different approaches to psychology, particularly useful for those interested in the history of psychology and those wishing to explore behaviourist and humanistic psychology in depth.

Mayhew, J. (1997) *Psychological Change, A Practical Introduction*, Basingstoke: Macmillan. A detailed but very user-friendly overview of behaviourist, psychodynamic and humanistic psychology, including major theories and their applications. Because of the emphasis on psychology applied to the caring professions, this is particularly useful for those studying psychology as part of training in nursing, social work and teaching.

Tavris, C. and Wade, C. (1997) *Psychology in Perspective*, New York: Longman. Probably the best general text on different psychological perspectives. Covers all the perspectives treated in this text in greater detail.

2

Behavioural psychology

Key assumptions of the approach

In 1948, B.F. Skinner placed eight pigeons in specially designed boxes (now known as Skinner boxes). On one wall was a pad which the pigeons could peck. The box also contained a food dispenser which could be controlled by the experimenter. In previous studies pigeons had learned to obtain food by pecking the pad – i.e. whenever they pecked the pad the food dispenser would produce a food pellet. In this study Skinner adjusted the food dispenser to administer food every 15 seconds regardless of what the pigeons did. Skinner discovered that six of the eight birds responded by adopting repetitive and unusual behaviours. One bird hopped up and down for its food, another bobbed its head repeatedly. When Skinner adjusted the food dispenser to administer food more slowly the head-bobbing bird increased the speed of its head movement. Skinner proposed that he had created 'superstitious' pigeons. Because food had followed head-bobbing or hopping, the birds had come to learn that food would always follow that behaviour. Being motivated by food, they repeated the behaviour constantly!

Looking at Skinner's classic study of the superstitious pigeons we can draw out some of the major features of behavioural psychology:

- *Psychology should be seen as a science, to be studied in a scientific manner*. Skinner's study of superstitious behaviour in pigeons was conducted under carefully controlled laboratory conditions.
- *Behaviourism is primarily concerned with observable behaviour, as opposed to internal events like thinking and emotion*. Note that Skinner did not claim to have created superstitious *beliefs* in the pigeons or say that the birds learnt to bob or hop because they *wanted* food. He instead concentrated on describing the easily observed behaviour that the pigeons acquired.
- *The major influence on human behaviour is learning from our environment*. In the Skinner study, because food followed a particular behaviour the birds learned (wrongly) to repeat that behaviour.
- *There is little difference between the learning that takes place in humans and that in other animals, therefore research can be carried out on animals as well as on humans*. Skinner proposed that the way humans learn superstitious behaviour is much the same as the way the pigeons learned to hop or bob.

If your layperson's idea of psychology has always been of people in laboratories wearing white coats and watching hapless rats try to negotiate mazes in order to get to their dinner, then you are probably thinking of behavioural psychology. Behaviourism and its offshoots tend to be among the most scientific of the psychological perspectives. The emphasis of behavioural psychology is on how we *learn* to behave in certain ways. We are all constantly learning new behaviours and how to modify our existing behaviour. Behavioural psychology is the psychological approach that focuses on how this learning takes place.

In this chapter we can look at the two major types of learning proposed by behaviourists – classical and operant conditioning – and a more recent offshoot of behaviourism – social learning. We can then look at how behavioural principles can be applied to change people's behaviour, and use behavioural principles to try to understand the problem of media violence.

Classical conditioning and early behavioural theory

Like many great scientific advances, classical conditioning was discovered accidentally. The nineteenth-century Russian physiologist Ivan Pavlov (Pavlov, [1856] 1927) was looking at salivation in dogs in response to being fed, when he noticed that his dogs would begin to salivate whenever he entered the room, even when he was not bringing them food. At first this was something of a nuisance (not to mention messy!). However, when Pavlov discovered that any object or event which the dogs learnt to associate with food (such as the food bowl) would trigger the same response, he realised that he had made an important discovery, and he devoted the rest of his career to studying this type of learning.

Classical conditioning involves learning to associate a stimulus that already brings about a particular response with a new stimulus, so that the new stimulus brings about the same response. Pavlov developed some rather unfriendly technical terms to describe this process. The **unconditioned stimulus** (or US) is the object or event that originally produces the response. The response to this is called the **unconditioned response** (or UR). The **neutral stimulus** (NS) is a new stimulus that does not produce a response. Once the neutral stimulus has become associated with the unconditioned stimulus, it becomes a **conditioned stimulus** (CS). The **conditioned response** (CR) is the response to the conditioned stimulus. If that sounds rather like a tongue-twister, you may find that Figure 2.1, which explains how Pavlov's dogs learned to salivate in response to the sight of their food bowl, makes things a little clearer.

Imagine that you are afraid of dogs and you have just been bitten by a large, vicious dog whilst waiting for a bus. You then find that you have developed an irrational fear of bus stops. Explain this using the principles of classical conditioning. You may find it helps to draw up a three-stage model like Figure 2.1.

Progress exercise

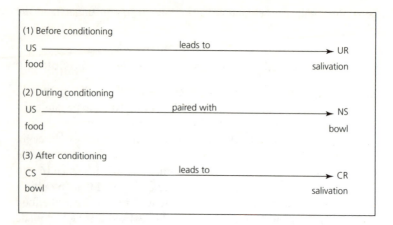

Figure 2.1 **The process of classical conditioning in Pavlov's dogs**

Behaviourism as a movement in psychology appeared in 1913 when John Broadus Watson published the classic article 'Psychology as the behaviourist views it'. Watson believed that all individual differences in behaviour were due to different experiences of learning. He famously said:

> Give me a dozen healthy infants, well-formed, and my own specified world to bring them up in and I'll guarantee to take any one at random and train him to become any type of specialist I might select – doctor, lawyer, artist, merchant-chief and, yes, even beggar-man and thief, regardless of his talents, penchants, tendencies, abilities, vocations and the race of his ancestors.
>
> (Watson, 1925, p. 104)

Watson (1919) proposed that the process of classical conditioning was able to explain all aspects of human psychology. Everything from speech to emotional responses were simply patterns of stimulus and response. Watson denied completely the existence of the mind or consciousness. Emotions were regarded simply as conditioned bodily responses to outside events. Thinking was explained simply as talking quietly. If you are wondering how Watson thought he had come to these conclusions without a mind, he would presumably have replied that they were the inevitable result of a complex and most fortunate set of conditioning experiences! Watson demonstrated learning by classical conditioning in humans in the classic study of Little Albert.

KEY STUDY: J.B. Watson and R. Rayner (1920) Conditioned emotional responses. *Journal of Experimental Psychology* **3, 1–14.**

Aim: The researchers aimed to demonstrate that classical conditioning could be used to create a fear response in a child to an innocuous stimulus (one that we would not normally expect to frighten children). By doing this Watson and Rayner hoped to show that human behaviour could be accounted for by the process of classical conditioning.

Method: A laboratory experiment was carried out using a single participant, a male infant aged nine months at the start of the study. Albert Little, or 'Little Albert' as he has become known, was judged to be particularly emotionally stable. Albert was assessed on his responses to a number of objects, including a white rat, and he displayed no fear. In fact he wanted to play with the rat. In classical conditioning terms, the rat was a *neutral stimulus* because it did not produce a fear response. Two months later Little Albert was again presented with the white rat. This time, when he reached for it, the researchers struck a four-foot metal bar just behind his ear, making a loud noise and frightening Albert. The sound of the bar being banged was an *unconditioned stimulus* because it elicited a fear response from the start. The procedure was repeated five times a week later and twice more 17 days later. Albert's responses to the rat plus the loud noise, to the rat alone and to other white fluffy objects were noted.

Results: In the first trial when the metal bar was struck, Albert displayed some distress, jumping violently and sticking his face into a mattress. In the second trial, Albert was suspicious of the rat, and by the next session he leaned away from the rat as soon as it was presented. When a rabbit was placed next to him, Albert cried. Seven weeks later Albert cried in response to a variety of white furry objects including a fur coat and a Father Christmas beard. This response to objects that reminded Albert of the conditioned stimulus is called **generalisation**.

Discussion

This is a classic study, and clearly demonstrates that it is possible to artificially induce emotional responses by classical conditioning. It was intended that Little Albert would be deconditioned, but he was adopted and his adoptive mother (understandably) refused to let Watson experiment further. Fortunately, conditioned responses tend to decline with time – this is called **extinction** – so we may hope that Albert lived a relatively normal life and developed a healthy affection for small animals and Father Christmas. That said, there is no doubt that this study would be unacceptable by modern ethical standards. Albert was not capable of giving informed consent to take part in the study, nor could he withdraw if he wished. He was subjected to discomfort and distress, and researchers were unsure about possible long-term effects. Of course in the 1920s there were no published ethical guidelines for psychologists to follow, and people held scientists in more esteem than is usual today and so tended not to question their actions.

Evaluation of early behavioural theory

There is no doubt that classical conditioning exists, nor that it can be an important mechanism in human learning. Watson made a huge contribution to psychology by showing how classical conditioning can account for human learning. To those who see psychology as a pure science, Watson did us a great service by forcing researchers to become more scientific. It goes without saying that those who do not see psychology as a pure science hold rather less affection for Watson!

There are, however, a number of criticisms that can be applied to Watson's work. He certainly overplayed the importance of classical conditioning. Later behaviourists introduced us to other forms of learning, and other approaches to psychology have shown us that learning of behaviour is not sufficient explanation of the complexities of human psychology. If you found Watson's assertion that there is no such thing as a human mind rather extreme (let's face it, if you are able to think about it, you are using your mind and so it *must* be wrong), then you are not alone. Almost none of us would now subscribe to this view, and modern psychology sees thinking and emotion as every bit as important as behaviour.

Operant conditioning and later behavioural theory

By the 1920s Watson had left academic psychology (he married his assistant Rosalie Raynor and became an advertising executive), and other behaviourists were becoming influential, proposing new forms of learning other than classical conditioning. Perhaps the most important of these was Burrhus Frederic Skinner (he understandably preferred to be known as B.F. Skinner). Skinner's views were slightly less extreme than those of Watson. Skinner believed that we do have such a thing as a mind, but that it is simply more productive to study observable behaviour rather than internal mental events. Skinner believed that the best way to understand a behaviour is to look at the causes of an action and its consequences. He called this approach **radical behaviourism** in order to distinguish his theory from the stimulus–response approach of Watson.

Operant conditioning

Whereas classical conditioning depends on developing associations between events, operant conditioning involves learning from the consequences of our behaviour. Skinner was not the first psychologist to study learning by consequences. Thorndike (1898) studied learning in cats. He placed cats in a cage, just out of reach of which was a scrap of fish. The cats experimented with different ways to escape the cage and reach the fish. Eventually they would stumble upon the lever which opened the cage. In successive trials the cats would learn that pressing the lever would have favourable consequences and they would adopt this behaviour, becoming increasingly quick at pressing the lever.

Building upon the work of Thorndike, Skinner (1938) distinguished two types of behaviour. **Respondent behaviour** is based on reflexes and does not require learning. For example, if you touch a hot surface, you will quickly remove your hand. **Operant behaviour**, however, is learnt, and is performed spontaneously rather than as an automatic response to a situation. According to Skinner, most human behaviour is operant. Skinner identified three types of response or **operant** that can follow a behaviour:

*   **neutral operants**: responses from the environment that neither increase nor decrease the probability of the behaviour being repeated;

17

- **reinforcers**: responses from the environment that increase the probability being repeated;
- **punishers**: responses from the environment that decrease the probability being repeated.

Figure 2.2 **The author's cat has learnt that food often follows looking cute**

We can all think of examples of how our own behaviour has been affected by reinforcers and punishers. As a child you probably tried out a number of behaviours and learnt from their consequences. For example, if when you were younger you tried smoking at school, and the chief consequence was that you got in with the crowd you always wanted to hang out with, you would have been *reinforced* and would be likely to repeat the behaviour. If, however, the main consequence was that you were caught, caned, suspended from school and your parents became involved you would most certainly have been *punished*, and you would consequently be much less likely to smoke now. Note however that whether the outcome is a punisher or a reinforcer depends on the outcome. If the main outcome of being caught was hero status with your peers then being caught would be a reinforcer not a punisher.

Progress exercise

Marcus Cole, hero of the cult science-fiction series *Babylon 5*, famously said 'I always said you can get further with a kind word and a big stick than you can with just a kind word.' Explain this advice in terms of operant conditioning.

Positive and negative reinforcement

Some behaviours are reinforced because they bring about a pleasant consequence. This is called **positive reinforcement**. Others are reinforced because they eliminate something unpleasant. This is called **negative reinforcement**. A good example of positive and negative reinforcement lies in our everyday use of drugs. You may have drunk alcohol for pleasure and you may have taken aspirin or paracetamol to relieve a headache. The effects of alcohol are physically pleasant, therefore when we drink it we are *positively reinforced*. The use of aspirin and paracetamol, on the other hand, become *negatively reinforced* when they remove headaches. Because of this reinforcement, we can easily get into the habit of taking both alcohol and pain-killers.

Positive and negative punishment

Just like reinforcers, punishers can be positive or negative. A **positive punisher** is an unpleasant stimulus, whilst a **negative punisher** is the removal of a pleasurable stimulus. Those of us who were once naughty children probably received a number of positive and negative punishments. Positive punishers include shouting, scolding and spanking. Negative punishment might involve the removal of attention, for example by sending the child to their room, or it might mean removing pocket-money or 'grounding' them. We shall look more closely at the management of children's behaviour later in this chapter.

Uncontrollable reinforcers

The principles of operant conditioning predict that if an effect consistently follows an action, we will learn that our action caused that effect, regardless of whether or not it was actually our behaviour that led to the effect. Positive consequences that occur regardless of our actions are called **uncontrollable reinforcers**. This is exactly what Skinner demonstrated in his superstitious pigeon study. More recently Matute (1996) demonstrated the same phenomenon in humans by making the computers of working students emit irritating noises. Students tended to try to stop the noise, for example by pressing buttons. Actually the computers stopped emitting the noise automatically (the cessation of the noise was thus an uncontrollable reinforcer), but because the students always tried to stop it, the stopping of the noise always followed their actions. They thus 'learnt' that they could stop the noise by pressing buttons. When a different group of students were told not to try to stop the noise they learnt that they could not stop it but that it would stop spontaneously.

Matute (1998) has suggested that similar processes occur outside the psychology laboratory, for example when people have to deal with untreatable medical conditions. People might acknowledge that they have little control over the situation, but this is likely to lead to depression. Alternatively they might try a range of treatments and, if a recovery occurs, they might associate this with a particular treatment, however unlikely that particular treatment was to have worked. This can lead to the patient having an irrational (or superstitious) belief in the treatment. This in turn can have both positive and negative consequences. The patient may be less likely to become depressed but also less likely to use orthodox medical services.

Evaluation of radical behaviourism

Skinner's radical behaviourism took psychology considerably further forward than did the early behaviourism of Watson. Operant *and* classical conditioning together can account for a far wider range of psychological phenomena than classical conditioning alone. The principle of reinforcement is one of the most powerful tools in psychology, and has been successfully applied across a huge range of situations, including psychological therapy, education and child-rearing. To the hard-nosed scientists among us, Skinner has maintained the pure-science tradition begun by Watson, whilst avoiding some of his crass oversimplifications. Operant conditioning also provides a good explanation of how, in everyday life, we are constantly influenced by our environment.

This is not to say that Skinner has had it all his own way. Many psychologists, including those from the cognitive school, would disagree with Skinner that we can learn everything we need to know about psychology from observable behaviour, and instead prefer to focus on the study of mental events. Most would also say that, whilst studying operant conditioning can teach us about learning, learning *alone* cannot explain all aspects of human behaviour and experience. Skinner probably underestimated the importance of biological factors, including the influence of genetic differences and instincts on behaviour.

Social learning theory

Not all behaviourists accepted Skinner's belief that all behaviour was learned by direct reinforcement. Dollard and Miller (1950) were the first rebels to use the term 'social learning' to describe the processes by which we learn behaviour through observing others. The idea of social learning was developed into a major theory by Albert Bandura (1978).

Bandura agreed with Skinner that much of our behaviour is acquired through operant conditioning, but he saw the *main* influence on behaviour as the result of imitating the behaviour of a **model**. Bandura *et al.* (1961) demonstrated the tendency of children to imitate adult behaviour in a classic study.

KEY STUDY: A. Bandura *et al.* (1961) Transmission of aggression through imitation of aggressive models. *Journal of Abnormal and Social Psychology* 63 (3), 575–582.

Aim: The researchers aimed to demonstrate that social behaviours can be acquired by imitation. They chose to focus on aggression because this is a relatively easy category of behaviour to observe. The main hypothesis being tested was that children exposed to models behaving aggressively will be more likely to behave aggressively than children not exposed to aggressive models. Researchers were also interested in whether children were more likely to imitate same-sex models and whether there was an overall sex-difference in levels of aggression.

Method: 36 boys and 36 girls were divided into groups. An independent measures design was used because once children had participated in one condition it was likely that their behaviour would be altered for the remainder of the experiment. Twenty-four children formed a control group whilst the remaining 48 were divided into six groups, three male and three female. The children in each group were matched for individual differences in aggression. The six groups were exposed to either a same-sex adult or an opposite-sex adult behaving either aggressively or non-aggressively. The participants observed the model assembling toys in a room with a large inflatable Bobo doll. In the non-aggressive condition the model ignored the Bobo doll, whilst in the aggressive condition the model punched and kicked the doll and hit it with a hammer, while making aggressive comments such as 'sock him in the nose'. The children were then taken one at a time to a different room containing several toys including a Bobo doll. Their behaviour was then watched through a two-way mirror.

Results: The main research hypothesis was accepted. There was very little aggression displayed towards the Bobo doll by children who had not been exposed to the aggressive behaviour of the adult (70 per cent displayed no aggression at all), whilst there was a high level of aggression on the part of children who had witnessed the aggressive behaviour. Overall, boys displayed higher levels of physical aggression but no higher levels of verbal aggression. Interestingly, boys were more likely to imitate both physical and verbal aggression from male models. Girls however were more likely to imitate verbal aggression from female models but no more likely to imitate physical aggression.

Discussion

This study clearly demonstrates that at least some aspects of children's social behaviour are influenced by witnessing the social behaviour of others. It is also a good example of a well-controlled laboratory experiment. The idea that children tend to imitate modelled behaviour has important implications, particularly in respect of the argument about media violence. We can return to this issue later in the chapter. Follow-up studies have shown that reinforcement is also important in social learning. When children witnessed the model being rewarded for aggression towards the Bobo doll, the rates of aggression in children were even higher. This type of 'second-hand' reinforcement is called **vicarious reinforcement**.

As well as stressing the importance of imitation of behaviour, Bandura's social learning approach differs from earlier behavioural theories in other ways. Bandura *et al*. (1963) demonstrated that reinforcement can be *vicarious* (see the discussion section in the key study). This means that we learn from seeing others being reinforced. Bandura suggested that in order to learn this way, we must process the information about the consequences of people's actions and come to logical conclusions about whether we should copy the behaviour. This reference to mental or *cognitive* processes was a departure from the traditional behaviourist position. Lundin (1996) has thus described Bandura's approach as 'soft behaviourism' (p. 233).

Bandura's acknowledgement of cognitive processes led him to a further departure from traditional behaviourism. Whereas radical behaviourists see us as reacting automatically to events, and hence being largely passive victims of our environment, social learning theorists see us as having a measure of control over the environment in which we find ourselves. For example, Bandura (1978) pointed out that although we may be influenced by television, *we choose what to watch* and thus largely shape our own behaviour as opposed to having it shaped for us.

Summarise the ways in which social learning theory and radical behaviourism differ. You might want to consider the main influences on behaviour, the nature of reinforcement and the role of cognitive processes.

Progress exercise

Evaluation of social learning theory

Bandura has maintained the behaviourists' tradition of rigorous experimental research, but has departed from some of their more restrictive ideas such as ignoring mental processes. He has also introduced us to imitation as a major influence on human behaviour.

To most psychologists these are positive developments and Bandura 'tells a more complete story' (Lundin, 1996, p. 233) than earlier behavioural theories. Social learning theory has proved useful in gaining an understanding of children's behaviour and has been invaluable in informing the debate over media violence (see pp. 26–28).

Critics of Bandura tend to come from two very different sources. Radical behaviourists have seen Bandura as nothing less than a traitor for daring to introduce mental processes to behavioural psychology. Others have challenged Bandura for not going far enough – social learning theory is rather sketchy on the details of *how* we influence our environment and make choices. Like all behavioural theories, social learning underplays some aspects of human learning and development that would be considered central by other perspectives (for example the role of emotion). We shall return to this issue when evaluating the behavioural approach as a whole.

Key application: behaviour change

Because the ultimate aim of behavioural psychology has always been to control behaviour, it comes as no surprise that behaviourists have developed powerful techniques to alter the patterns of people's behaviour. Whilst these techniques do have some rather sinister applications (see for example Banyard, 1999 in this series for a discussion), they can also be used benevolently in a number of situations. Psychologists can use classical conditioning techniques to reduce or remove the symptoms of phobias (see for example Cave, 1999 in this series), or to help to remove unwanted behaviours, such as paedophilia. Operant conditioning techniques can be used to help rehabilitate people such as long-term psychiatric patients who have been out of contact with 'normal' society for a while. Operant conditioning techniques can also be of use in helping parents regulate children's behaviour. The principles of social learning have been adapted to train people in social skills, for example how to behave on a date. Let us spend some time looking at two of these examples in a little more depth.

Aversion therapy

Rather like the way Watson and Rayner succeeded in inducing a fear response in Little Albert by classical conditioning, there are some circumstances in which contemporary psychologists deliberately condition patients to associate an aspect of their behaviour with a noxious stimulus, such as an electric shock or an emetic drug (which induces vomiting). This means that if they go to repeat the behaviour in the future they are vividly reminded of the noxious stimulus and are thus discouraged to go on and actually perform the behaviour. A graphic example of aversion therapy was depicted in Anthony Burgess's *A Clockwork Orange*, where a violent young man was 'rehabilitated' by being made to sit through films of violence whilst vomiting due to the effects of an emetic. The unfortunate man found that, once released, whenever he went to hit someone his conditioning kicked in and he threw up instead.

A real-life example of the use of aversion therapy comes from Marshall and Barbaree (1988). They taught child-molesters to administer themselves smelling salts whenever they had erotic thoughts involving children. They also used penile plethysmography to help condition the men out of attraction to children. This means that the men wore a pressure-sensitive penis-ring which, if stretched, would complete an electric circuit and administer a painful shock. They were shown pictures of children, and, whenever they responded physically they would receive a shock. The aim was that the men would begin to associate erotic thoughts of children with a noxious smell and electric shocks. At follow-up, 13 per cent of the treatment group reoffended as opposed to 34 per cent of a control group, showing that the aversion therapy was quite effective. This may sound like a rather barbaric procedure, but you should be aware that it was done with the consent of the offenders, who expressed a wish to change their behaviour. The aversion procedure was also accompanied by supportive counselling, so that as far as possible it was experienced as therapy rather than a punishment.

Child-behaviour management

Whether they know it or not, all those involved with children – most importantly parents – respond to all child behaviours with neutral, punishing or reinforcing operants. Sometimes parents and others can benefit from learning how to better use operants to regulate children's behaviour. Mayhew (1997) has suggested that behaviour management can be helpful when a child's behaviour is actually a problem and not part of normal development, and when the behaviour is well-established in the child as opposed to being elicited by a particular situation (such as an unreasonably harsh adult).

According to Mayhew, parents tend to overuse punishment to regulate children's behaviour, and this can cause difficulties. Punishment is inefficient for a number of reasons. Children learn what is wrong from punishment, but not what is *right*, and it causes resentment in the child. Furthermore, because the child is likely to be made either angry or afraid by punishment their levels of physical arousal will be very high and this inhibits learning. There is also a risk that the child will begin to associate the punishment not with their behaviour but with the person administering it, harming the parent–child relationship. Finally, if the child perceives that it gets attention when it misbehaves but is ignored when it behaves well, the attention inherent in punishment can become a positive reinforcer, and may actually increase the undesirable behaviour.

Parenting skills training involves teaching parents to reduce the use of punishment, and instead to focus on reinforcing appropriate behaviour. This may involve strategies as simple as ignoring tantrums (thus replacing the reinforcer of attention with a neutral operant) and actively rewarding good behaviour with attention and affection (thus replacing a neutral operant with a positive reinforcer). This emphasis on ignoring bad behaviour and rewarding good behaviour has also gained influence in schools, where it has become known as **positive discipline**. A slightly more advanced technique also based on operant conditioning is the **token economy**. Parents and teachers can reward good behaviour with tokens such as stars on a 'star-chart'. Stars are accumulated and the child may then be rewarded in some way, either after a fixed time interval or when a certain number of tokens have been accumulated.

Contemporary issue: the media violence debate

There has been much debate in recent years over the issue of violence in the media. This debate centres around the possibility that viewers, particularly children, may imitate aggressive behaviour witnessed on television and in films. In Britain the debate has hotted up since the tragic death in 1993 of toddler James Bulger at the hands of two 10-year-old children, who had allegedly watched a number of violent videos. From a social learning perspective, as children acquire a repertoire of behaviour by imitating what they observe, media violence is likely to directly lead to violent behaviour. A slightly more sophisticated look at social learning theory would lead us to expect that not only are people likely to be influenced by media violence but also that those predisposed to violence will seek out violent material and reinforce their violent tendencies.

A study by Black and Bevan (1992) supports both these predictions. Researchers approached people either waiting in cinema queues or leaving the cinema after a film. Participants were asked to fill in a questionnaire asking them about their tendencies for violence. Participants waiting to see violent films reported significantly greater violent tendencies than those waiting to see non-violent films, supporting the social learning prediction that violent people seek out violent material. Those leaving the cinema after seeing violent films reported greater violent tendencies than those waiting to see violent films, supporting the social learning prediction that people's tendency for violence is increased by exposure to violent material. Those leaving non-violent films did not show a corresponding increase in violent tendencies.

There are of course methodological limitations with this and similar studies linking media violence to later aggression. The fact that the participants reported that they *would* be more violent is not the same as demonstrating that they actually *became* more violent. Moreover, they were surveyed immediately after watching the violent films. At this point they were likely to have had high levels of arousal triggered by the exciting films. We cannot assume that once these arousal levels had fallen they would continue to report the same violent tendencies.

Another source of evidence in the debate involves retrospectively looking at the viewing habits of convicted violent offenders. The evidence linking the murder of James Bulger to particular videos is not strong, but large-scale studies have found that a disproportionate number of offenders have a history of viewing violent material. For example Bailey (1993) looked at the history of 40 adolescent murders and 200 young sex offenders and concluded that their very heavy use of pornography and violent film material was likely to be a factor in their offending. Given however that people with a predisposition to violence probably seek out such material and would probably be violent to some extent anyway, untangling cause and effect from this type of data is very difficult. There is thus a limited body of evidence linking media violence to aggression in viewers, but it is unlikely that media violence is ever the *sole* cause of aggression.

An obvious question, given the evidence for a link between media violence and aggression in young people, but also given the limitations of the available evidence, concerns whether we should try to reduce aggression in society by censorship. Given that people predisposed to violence would be highly motivated to obtain violent material, censorship of all violent material would have to be extremely thorough to be effective. There may however be a case for identifying and controlling material particularly likely to affect vulnerable individuals. For example the 1980s video nasty genre is particularly linked with associating cruelty with entertainment or amusement. There is also a tendency in this genre to make the viewer identify with the perpetrator of sadistic violence. This is in contrast to traditional horror where the viewer tends to identify with the victims.

Contributions and limitations of behavioural psychology

- At least to the hard-nosed scientists amongst us, the behavioural approach to psychology is generally regarded as 'good, solid stuff'. Theories are easily testable and they are backed by a large body of rigorous experimental research (of course this means little to those who reject the idea of psychology as science).
- As well as being academically sound, behavioural principles can easily be applied in the real world to understand everyday situations such as why a child tends to have more tantrums if it gets them more attention. Tavris and Wade (1997) have pointed out that behaviourism has taught us that we all influence each other all the time, even when we don't realise it.
- Behavioural psychology can also be applied by psychologists in a huge range of situations with powerful effects. Applications range from therapies for a variety of psychological conditions to child behaviour management, understanding the effects of media violence, encouraging health-promoting behaviours, advertising and marketing products and improving the effectiveness of penal systems, to name just a few.

- One reason why behavioural psychology is so practical is that it emphasises the capacity of people to change, given an appropriate learning environment. Whilst there may be genetic differences between individuals, that line of enquiry can sometimes lead to defeatist attitudes because it emphasises what does not change. A behavioural perspective, by contrast, is optimistic and readily lends itself to giving people practical help because it emphasises what can change. This means that it is a liberation philosophy, encouraging a view of all people as equal.

You might ask why, given these major contributions to psychology, the behavioural approach arouses hostility from so many non-behavioural psychologists. Each school of psychology would give you a different specific answer, but they would probably all identify much the same underlying problems:

- The behavioural approach is **reductionist**. This means that it *reduces* the complexity of human behaviour to a few simple principles of learning. Thus from a cognitive perspective, behavioural psychology largely ignores the importance of higher mental processes such as decision-making.
- From a psychodynamic perspective, behavioural approaches ignore the importance of relationships, and the *dynamics* of families and groups within which learning takes place. From a biological perspective, behavioural psychology underplays the importance of evolution, genetics and brain physiology on behaviour.
- There are also more philosophical concerns about adopting a behavioural viewpoint. Many, particularly those from the humanistic school, would say that behaviourism is mechanistic and cannot explain human capacity for free will and achievement.
- The aims of behavioural psychology – to predict and control behaviour – are also regarded with some suspicion by many psychologists. In this chapter we have focused on positive uses of behavioural techniques, but such techniques lend themselves equally easily to torture, brainwashing and political oppression. Kohn (1993) has objected to the culture of behaviourism in the workplace, comparing the regimes of reward and punishment with those used by Skinner with his rats.

Summary

Behavioural psychology is a highly successful and influential perspective, which emphasises the importance of learning behaviour by classical and operant conditioning, and by social learning. The approach places great emphasis on testable concepts and rigorous experimental research. Behavioural psychology has many applications, centring around powerful techniques for changing people's behaviour. Although these techniques remain very important in psychology, the limitations of behaviourism in its pure form are now apparent, and relatively few psychologists still describe themselves as pure behaviourists.

Review exercise

Look back at the three vignettes in Chapter 1. Now that you know a little more about the behavioural approach, reflect on how well behavioural theory explains each of these scenarios. You may find it helpful to note down what aspects of each situation a behavioural approach can explain fully, and where it runs into some difficulties.

Further reading

Matute, H. (1998) The learning perspective, in M. Eysenck (ed.) *Psychology: An Integrated Approach*, Harlow: Addison-Wesley Longman. A very detailed and up-to-date account of a range of learning theories.

Skinner, B.F. (1974) *About Behaviourism*, London: Jonathan Cape. There is nothing like hearing it straight from the horse's mouth! It is particularly interesting to see how Skinner refutes many of the criticisms often made of behaviourism, including those in this chapter.

Tavris, C. and Wade, C. (1997) *Psychology in Perspective*, New York: Addison-Wesley Longman. Includes a more advanced and detailed general overview and evaluation of behavioural psychology than is possible here, including applications to child-care, education and therapy.

3

Psychodynamic psychology

- Key assumptions of the approach
- Freud's theories
- Winnicott's theories
- Key application: mental health
- Contemporary issue: why do we love monsters?
- Contributions and limitations of the psychodynamic approach
- Summary

Key assumptions of the approach

Have you ever had the experience of doing something out of character such as taking an instant dislike to a stranger, or forgetting to go to an appointment that was important but which you were secretly dreading? If you have, then the chances are that you were influenced by *unconscious* mental processes – i.e. wishes, emotions, etc. of which you were not aware. You might for example have disliked the stranger because they reminded you of someone else, or forgotten the appointment because you simply did not want to go. The psychodynamic approach is an approach to psychology which emphasises these unconscious processes. The way in which a psychodynamic psychologist might look at unconscious processes is well-illustrated by the case of Alex, described by Lemma-Wright (1995).

Alex was the older of two sisters. She loved her sister dearly, but had always resented her a little, believing that her family had always doted on her sister while ignoring her. As a child Alex had once become so angry with her sister for being the centre of attention that she dragged her into the sea, frightening her badly. As an adult, Alex frequently found herself feeling obliged to organise things for her sister and to help her out of financial difficulties. One weekend Alex organised a sea boat-trip to celebrate her sister's birthday. The trip went well, but Alex suffered a panic attack on the boat. She had no idea why until a few days later she had a dream in which she had a fight with a friend (who reminded her of her sister) and wished her dead. It then became clear that the boat-trip, in which Alex had once again taken her sister into the sea, had stirred up guilty memories of the time she had dragged her into the sea.

A common-sense approach might reveal no obvious connections between Alex's childhood memories, her panic attack and her dream. A psychodynamic psychologist however would look beyond the obvious to see whether there are any possible connections between events. Looking at the case of Alex, we can pick out some of the assumptions underlying psychodynamic psychology:

- *Our behaviour and feelings as adults (including psychological problems) are rooted in our childhood experiences.* For Alex, the crucial childhood experiences seem to be of feeling ignored by her parents and reacting by becoming aggressive to her sister.
- *Relationships (especially parenting) are of primary importance in determining how we feel and behave.* In Alex's case, her difficulties appear to be rooted in her relationship with her parents and her sister.
- *Our behaviour and feelings are powerfully affected by the meaning of events to the unconscious mind, and by unconscious motives.* Although consciously, Alex thought she was taking her sister to sea for a birthday treat, the event seems to have quite a different meaning to her unconscious mind. We might even wonder whether Alex was motivated on an unconscious level to take her sister to sea again in order to kill her.

- In contrast to other branches of psychology which place a strong emphasis on systematic, scientific research, *psycho-dynamic psychology looks for information in dreams, symptoms, irrational behaviour and what patients say in therapy.*

(Adapted from Rycroft, 1968; Tavris and Wade, 1997; Jarvis, 2000)

If you know very little about psychology, and you have heard of just one psychologist, the chances are that this is Sigmund Freud, the founder of the psychodynamic approach to psychology, or **psychoanalysis**. If Freud (or at least Freud as he is popularly portrayed) represents your layperson's idea of psychology then you probably have an image of a patient lying on a couch talking about their deepest and darkest secrets. In deliberate contrast to behavioural psychology, examined in Chapter 2, psychodynamic psychology ignores the trappings of science and instead focuses on trying to get 'inside the head' of individuals in order to make sense of their relationships, experiences and how they see the world.

In this chapter we can look at the work of Freud and that of one other influential psychoanalyst, Donald Winnicott. We can then look at how psychodynamic principles have been applied in the field of mental health, and use them to try to understand the popularity of monsters, a seemingly irrational phenomenon common throughout history and common to many cultures.

Freud's theories

Sigmund Freud (writing between the 1890s and the 1930s) developed a collection of theories which have formed the basis of the psychodynamic approach to psychology. His theories are clinically derived – i.e. based on what his patients told him during therapy. Freud theorised on a wide variety of topics and developed his ideas throughout the period of his writing. It is not possible to overview all or most of Freud's ideas in this chapter, but we can look briefly at a few of Freud's more important contributions.

The unconscious mind and personality

Perhaps Freud's single most enduring and important idea was that the human personality has more than one aspect. We reveal this when we say things like 'part of me wants to do it, but part of me is afraid to'. Freud described his approach as 'depth psychology' and compared himself to an archaeologist digging away layers of the human mind. In his early **topographical model** Freud distinguished between the conscious mind, which consists of all the mental processes of which we are aware, the preconscious mind, which contains memories that can be recalled to consciousness under certain circumstances and the true unconscious mind, which contains our biologically based instincts, most importantly the primitive urges for sex and aggression. While we are fully aware of what is going on in the conscious mind, our feelings, motives and decisions are actually powerfully influenced by our past experiences, stored in the preconscious and instincts from the unconscious.

Freud believed that the influences of the preconscious and unconscious reveal themselves in a variety of ways, including dreams, apparent accidents, myths and stories and in slips of the tongue, now popularly known as 'Freudian slips'. Freud (1920) gave an example of such a slip when a British Member of Parliament referred to a colleague with whom he was irritated as 'the honourable member from Hell' instead of from Hull. A more recent example of a Freudian slip comes from a psychology student who, when telling the class how much she fancied William Shatner (who played Captain Kirk in *Star Trek*), accidentally referred to him instead as 'Captain Cock'.

Freud (1933) developed a further model of the personality, which has become known as the **structural model**. Building upon the idea that we frequently feel that a part of us wants to do something, whilst another part does not, Freud proposed a *dissection of the personality* into three parts, *it, I* and *above-I*, each of which represents a different aspect of the person and plays a different role in deciding on a course of action. *It* represents the amoral and instinctive aspect of the personality, present from birth. *It* wants to be satisfied, and *it* does not willingly tolerate delay or denial of its wishes. *I* is the aspect of the person that is aware of both the demands of *it* and the outside world, and which makes decisions. *I* develops through experience of dealing with the world, and develops the capacity to think logically. *Above-I* is the aspect of the personality formed from the influence of authority figures such as the parent, which poses restrictions on what actions are allowable. *Above-I* can reward the person with pride and punish with guilt according to whether they go along with its restrictions. You may come across these three aspects of the personality in further reading as the *id* (it), the *ego* (I) and the *superego* (above-I). Freud did not however use these terms – they were added by his translators in an attempt to make the theory appear more scientific. The terms 'It', 'I' and 'above-I', although slightly awkward, describe better the idea Freud meant to put across – the feeling that we are pulled in different directions by different influences (Bettelheim, 1985; Jacobs, 1992). Tavris and Wade (1997) have used an old joke to illustrate the relationship between the three aspects of the personality: 'The id says "I want, and I want it now"; the superego says "You can't have it; it's bad for you" and the ego, the rational mediator, says, "Well, maybe you can have some of it – later."'

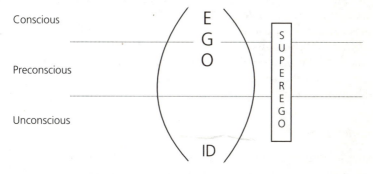

Figure 3.1 **Freud's topographical and structural models**
Source: After Freud (1933)

Evaluation of Freud's models of personality

The distinction between unconscious and conscious mental processes has stood the test of time, and forms an important part of contemporary research into motivation (see Harris and Campbell's key study later in this chapter, pp. 46–47). The distinction between the conscious, preconscious and unconscious has provided a useful way of thinking about the possible influences of instincts and past experience on our current feelings and behaviour. Real-life phenomena like Freudian slips demonstrate the reality of unconscious influences. However, to other psychologists determined to be scientific in their approach the concept of the unconscious mind has proved a source of considerable frustration because it defies objective description and is extremely difficult to test or measure. Some psychologists, particularly those from the humanistic tradition (see Chapter 4), are also somewhat offended by the idea that, like animals, we are ultimately motivated by sexual and aggressive instincts.

Freud saw the 'structural' model as having two major advantages over the topographical model. First, it provided an explanation for the experience of being pulled in different directions by different aspects of the self when making decisions, especially decisions with moral implications. Second, the *above-I* aspect of personality is useful in showing how relationships with others affect our personality. Someone with a harsh and punitive upbringing is thus likely to feel guilty a lot of the time – because the *above-I* aspect of their personality is powerful and punitive. Numerous psychologists from more scientific backgrounds have commented on the lack of any objective way in which to isolate, measure and study the *id, ego* and *superego*. However, this attitude probably fails to understand what Freud intended when he 'dissected' the personality – he was not literally dividing the mind into three parts, but describing the *experience* of being pulled in different directions by conflicting influences.

The ego-defences

One important aspect of Freudian theory which has become fully integrated into both everyday speech and mainstream psychology is the idea of ego-defences. These are unconscious mechanisms by which we protect ourselves from painful or guilty thoughts and feelings. You may for example have heard of *denial*, which occurs when smokers refuse to admit to themselves that they are endangering their lives by smoking, or *regression*, in which we use childlike strategies like crying helplessly or heading for the sweet-shop in order to comfort ourselves when under stress. The following are some of the other major Freudian defence mechanisms:

- *Repression* occurs when a memory, such as that of a traumatic event or a guilt-provoking sexual fantasy, is forcibly blocked from being remembered. We thus have no conscious recollection of the event or fantasy, although the memory may exert a powerful influence on us, sometimes leading to serious symptoms. Bateman and Holmes (1995) gave an example of repression in a man who came for therapy for depression. When talking about the death of his mother many years earlier, he suddenly remembered – for the first time as an adult – that his mother had committed suicide. Once he had retrieved this memory his symptoms lessened.

- *Reaction formation* takes place when we go a stage beyond denial and adopt an attitude that is diametrically opposed to our real feelings. The classic example is in **homophobia**, in which people who worry that they might have homosexual feelings deal with the resulting anxiety by adopting a harsh anti-homosexual attitude which helps convince themselves of their heterosexuality.
- *Displacement* takes place when we redirect emotions, most commonly anger, away from those who have caused them on to a third party. Displacement is easy to see in everyday life – most of us tend to take out our bad moods on unfortunate colleagues, friends and family, even when they were not the cause of the bad mood. Displacement can have more serious consequences however. One psychodynamic perspective on racial violence is that those who have had harsh, violent parenting, and who thus carry anger that they dare not express to their parents, look for a convenient target for their anger.
- *Sublimation* takes place when we manage to displace our emotions into constructive rather than destructive activity. This might for example be artistic – many great artists and musicians have had unhappy lives and have used the medium of art or music to express themselves. Sport is another example of putting our emotions into something constructive.

Evaluation of Freudian ego-defences

The general principle of the ego-defences is probably the most widely accepted of Freud's ideas, and they have proved useful in understanding a range of psychological phenomena. One recent study for example supported the idea that homophobia is due to reaction-formation. Adams *et al.* (1996) gave heterosexual men a test designed to classify them as either homophobic or non-homophobic. The two groups were then shown videos of either heterosexual, lesbian or male homosexual sex. Sexual arousal was measured in each case using a plethysmograph – see Chapter 2 (and this is the last time I will mention plethysmographs!). Homophobic and non-homophobic men did not differ in their responses to the lesbian or heterosexual scenes, but there was a significant difference when watching the male homosexual scenes. Eighty per cent of the homophobic men became sexually aroused as opposed to only 33 per cent of the non-homophobic men, clearly indicating that the homophobic men had a greater tendency towards homosexual arousal.

Freud believed that the most important of the defence mechanisms was repression. Of all the defence mechanisms, repression is the most controversial in contemporary psychology, and the issue of repression has become a bitter battlefield between psychodynamic practitioners and memory researchers. Memory researchers (e.g. Loftus, 1995) have pointed out that there is no direct evidence that repression exists. However, memory researchers favour *experimental* research – i.e. putting someone in a particular controlled situation and systematically noting what occurs in those circumstances. For ethical reasons memory researchers have not been able to recreate the traumatic conditions in which repression is alleged to occur. Psychodynamic psychologists would therefore argue that we simply would not expect to see the type of direct evidence for repression that memory researchers would find convincing. There are however innumerable case examples such as that given by Bateman and Holmes (see p. 37). There are also a number of **retrospective studies** which have looked back in time in an attempt to find out whether participants who remember traumatic incidents have ever forgotten them in the past. In one such study, Briere and Conte (1993) asked therapists who were treating adult patients who had reported childhood sexual abuse to ask the patients 'During the period of time between when the first forced sexual abuse happened and your 18th birthday, was there ever a time when you could not remember the forced sexual experience?' Fifty-nine per cent said yes, there had been a time when they had forgotten it. The problem with this type of study is that, just because patients had *forgotten* the experience, this does not necessarily mean that they had *repressed* it. This type of study therefore only provides indirect evidence for repression.

Which ego-defences might be being used in the following scenarios?

1   A student who is meant to be revising finds herself instead tidying her room.
2   A young athlete whose grandmother has just died finds himself training harder than usual.

Psychosexual development

Freud (1905) proposed that psychological development in childhood takes place in a series of fixed stages. These are called *psychosexual stages* because each stage represents the fixation of libido (roughly translated as sexual drives or instincts) on a different area of the body. If this sounds a little bizarre, it is important that you realise that Freud's use of the word 'sexual' was quite broad in meaning, and in his later writing (e.g. Freud, 1933) he put the word in quotation marks to emphasise that he did not mean that the child experiences these instincts as 'sexual' in the adult sense, but rather as a general physical experience. Libido is manifested in childhood as **organ-pleasure**, which centres on a different organ in each of the first three stages of development.

In the *oral stage* (the first year of life), while the child is suckling, the focus of organ-pleasure is the mouth. As well as taking nourishment through the mouth, children in the oral stage are taking comfort and their knowledge of the world via the mouth. Freud proposed that if the person becomes fixated in the oral stage, for example due to trauma, then they continue to display oral characteristics in adulthood. These can include habits such as thumb-sucking, smoking, tastes such as oral sex and attitudes such as *gullibility*, which represents the unquestioning taking in of information as children do in their first year.

In the *anal stage* (years 2–3), the focus of organ-pleasure now shifts to the anus. The child is now fully aware that they are a person in their own right and that their wishes can bring them into conflict with the demands of the outside world. Freud believed that this type of conflict tends to come to a head in potty-training, in which adults impose restrictions on when and where the child can defecate. The nature of this first conflict with authority can determine the child's future relationship with all forms of authority. Early or harsh potty-training can lead to the child becoming an anal-retentive personality who hates mess, is obsessively tidy, punctual and respectful of authority. Alternatively the child may turn out an anal-expulsive personality, who is messy, disorganised and rebellious.

In the *phallic stage* (years 3–6), the focus of organ-pleasure has shifted to the genitals, as the child becomes fully aware of its gender. This coincides with an awareness of the child's exclusion from some aspects of the parents' lives, such as sleeping in the same room. The resulting three-way relationship is known as the **Oedipus complex**, named after Oedipus, who, in a Greek legend, killed his father and married his mother (not realising who they were). In the Oedipus complex, a rivalry develops between the child and the same-sex parent for the affection of the opposite-sex parent. Freud believed that *on an unconscious level*, the child wishes to have sex with his mother and kill his father. This is not to suggest that children possess a conscious awareness of sexual intercourse or death in the adult sense. One of Freud's case-studies, Little Hans (Freud, 1909) illustrates the Oedipus complex.

KEY STUDY: S. Freud. (1909) Analysis of a phobia in a five-year-old boy. *Collected Papers* vol. III, 149–295.

Aim: Little Hans, a 5-year-old boy presented with a phobia of horses. Like all clinical case-studies, the primary aim was to treat the phobia. However, Freud's therapeutic input in this case was minimal, and a secondary aim was to explore what factors might have led to the phobia in the first place, and what factors led to its remission. By 1909 Freud's ideas about the Oedipus complex were well-established and Freud interpreted this case in line with his theory.

Case history: Freud's information about the course of Hans' condition was derived partially from observation of Hans himself, but mostly from Hans' father, who was familiar with Freud's work, and who gave him weekly reports. Hans' father reported that from the age of three, Hans had developed considerable interest in his 'widdler' and that at age 5 his mother had threatened to cut it off if he did not stop playing with it. At about the same time Hans developed a fear that a white horse would bite him. Hans' father reported that his fear seemed to be related to the horse's large penis. At the time Hans' phobia developed he was in the habit of getting into bed with his parents in the morning – something his father objected to. Hans' phobia got worse and he feared going out of the house in case he encountered a horse. He also suffered attacks of more generalised anxiety.

Over the next few weeks Hans' phobia gradually began to improve. His fear became limited to horses with black harnesses over their noses. Hans' father interpreted this as a reference to his moustache. The end of Hans' phobia of horses was accompanied by two significant fantasies which he told to his father. In the first, Hans had several imaginary children. When asked who their mother was, Hans replied 'Why, mummy, and you're their Grandaddy' (p. 238). In the second fantasy, which occurred the next day, Hans imagined that a plumber had come and fitted him with a bigger widdler. These fantasies marked the end of Hans' phobia.

Interpretation: Freud saw Hans' phobia as an expression of the Oedipus complex. Horses, particularly horses with black harnesses, symbolised his father. Horses were particularly suitable father-symbols because of their large penises. The fear began as an Oedipal conflict was developing around Hans being allowed in the parents' bed. Freud saw the Oedipus complex resolved as Hans fantasised himself with a big penis like his father's and married to his mother with his father present in the role of grandfather.

Discussion

The case of Little Hans does appear to provide support for Freud's theory of the Oedipus complex. However, there are difficulties with this type of evidence. Hans' father, who provided Freud with most of his data, was already familiar with the Oedipus complex and interpreted the case in the light of this. It is therefore possible that he supplied Hans with clues that led to his fantasies of marriage to his mother and his new large widdler. Of course even if Hans did have a fully fledged Oedipus complex, this shows that the Oedipus complex *exists* but not how *common* it is. Remember that Freud believed it to be universal.

Freud believed that the phallic stage was the most important of the developmental stages. When boys realise that they have a penis and girls do not, their unconscious response is **castration anxiety**, the belief that girls have already been castrated and the fear that they might be next! Their response is to repress their desire for the mother and identify with the father (in much the same way as we might identify with a bully and become like them in order to overcome our fear of them). Freud was somewhat perplexed by how girls dealt with the Oedipus complex on an unconscious level. He speculated (Freud, 1924) that when girls discover they lack a penis they feel that they have somehow come off worse, and are left with a sense of **penis envy**, the wish to have a penis. Penis envy is later sublimated into the wish to have a baby, and eventually relieved by actually having a baby.

Evaluation of psychosexual development

Freud's idea of infant 'sexuality' shocked the world when he published it, and remains every bit as controversial a century later, even though Freud did not say that children were sexually aware in an adult sense. The theory of psychosexual development is unquestionably the most unpopular part of Freud's work in modern psychology, and has been used repeatedly by critics to ridicule the psychodynamic approach as a whole. Feminist writers have objected vigorously (and understandably!) to Freud's speculation that women are motivated by feelings of inferiority because of their lack of a penis. If Freud is to be taken literally then this is quite justified. However Lacan (1966) has suggested that the idea of penis envy is not intended to be taken literally, but rather to mean envy of the penis as a *symbol of male dominance* in society. From Lacan's point of view, penis envy is not envy of the penis itself, but an awareness and resentment of the male-dominated society.

A balanced appraisal of Freud's psychosexual development comes from Brown and Pedder (1991). They proposed that Freud's labels of oral, anal and phallic were too narrow to describe what occurs in these stages. They suggested that we think of the oral stage as a stage of complete *dependency* on the caregiver(s), the anal stage as a period of *separation* from the caregiver and the phallic stage as a time of passionate emotions in which a *rivalry* may form between the child and the same-sex parent for the affection of the opposite-sex parent. The concepts of dependency, separation and rivalry are extremely useful in understanding the developing relationship between a child and its parents.

Dream theory

Freud famously called dreams 'the royal road to a knowledge of the activities of the unconscious mind' (Freud, 1900, p. 769). Dreams both perform important functions for the unconscious mind and serve as valuable clues to how the unconscious mind operates. On 24 July 1895, Freud had his own dream that was to form the basis of his theory. He had been worried about a patient, Irma, who was not doing as well in treatment as he had hoped. Freud in fact blamed himself for this, and was feeling guilty.

Freud dreamed that he met Irma at a party and examined her. He then saw a chemical formula for a drug that another doctor had given Irma flash before his eyes and realised that her condition was caused by a dirty syringe used by the other doctor. Freud's guilt was thus relieved.

Freud interpreted this dream as *wish-fulfilment*. He had wished that Irma's poor condition was not his fault and the dream had fulfilled this wish by informing him that another doctor was at fault. Based on this dream, Freud (1900) went on to propose that a major function of dreams was the fulfilment of wishes.

Freud elaborated this idea and distinguished between the manifest content of a dream (what the dreamer remembers) and the latent content (the underlying wish). The manifest content is often based upon the events of the day. The process whereby the underlying wish is translated into the manifest content is called **dream-work**. The purpose of dream-work is to transform the forbidden wish into a non-threatening form, thus reducing anxiety and allowing us to continue sleeping. Dream-work involves the processes of displacement, condensation and secondary elaboration.

Displacement takes place when we transform the person or object we are really concerned about to someone or something else. For example one of Freud's patients, who was extremely resentful of his sister-in-law and who used to refer to her as a dog, dreamed of strangling a small white dog. Freud interpreted this as representing his wish to kill his sister-in-law. You can imagine that, had he actually dreamed of killing his sister-in-law, the patient would probably have felt guilty. It appears that the unconscious mind, in transforming her into a dog, protected the dreamer from this guilt. *Condensation* takes place when we combine different factors into one aspect of the manifest content. Thus a woman who has angry feelings towards her husband and father might dream of punishing a man, who represents both the father and husband. *Secondary elaboration* is the final part of dream-work, and occurs when the unconscious mind strings together wish-fulfilling images into a logical succession of events, further obscuring the latent content. According to Freud this is why the manifest content of dreams can be in the form of plausible chains of events.

In Freud's later work on dreams he explored the possibility of universal symbols in dreams. Some of these were sexual in nature, including poles, guns and swords representing the penis and horse-riding and dancing representing sexual intercourse. However, Freud was cautious about these symbols and believed that in general symbols were personal rather than universal, and that one could not interpret what the manifest content of a dream symbolised without knowing about the person's circumstances. 'Dream dictionaries', which are still popular now, were a source of irritation to Freud. In an amusing example of the limitations of universal symbols, one of Freud's patients, after dreaming about holding a wriggling fish, said to him 'that's a Freudian symbol – it must be a penis!' Freud explored further and it turned out that the woman's mother, who was a passionate astrologer and a Pisces, was on the patient's mind because she disapproved of her daughter being in analysis. It seems more plausible, as Freud suggested, that the fish represented the patient's mother rather than a penis!

In his later work Freud recognised that there were other functions that could be performed by dreams apart from wish-fulfilment. Freud (1920) pointed out that following a traumatic event a common symptom is the reliving of the event in unconcealed and terrifying form in dreams. Freud saw this as an attempt to gain mastery over the trauma event and prevent it overwhelming the individual. Freud also recognised that not all dreams could be interpreted as serving the needs of the unconscious mind.

Evaluation of dream theory

According to Bateman and Holmes (1995), there has been a shift in the emphasis of psychodynamic thinking away from the *function* of dreams as wish-fulfilment towards looking at their *meaning* to the dreamer. According to Jung (1923), characters in dreams can represent different aspects of the person. This is now a more popular approach amongst psychodynamic therapists to the interpretation of dreams than wish-fulfilment.

More serious criticisms of Freud's dream theory come from psychologists of other theoretical backgrounds. Evans (1984) has proposed an alternative model of dreaming in which the main function is to organise and make sense of the day's events. However, Solms (1995) has noted that brain-damaged patients dream without their cognitive or physical deficits. Thus paralysed patients can move normally and aphasic patients (who have lost their language abilities) can speak. This suggests that dreaming may have more to do with wish-fulfilment than what happened to the patient that day.

Try keeping a dream-diary for a week. Record your dreams as soon as you wake up in the morning. Look at your dreams. Does it seem likely that they represent wish-fulfilment?

Progress exercise

Discussion of Freud's work

In this chapter we have only superficially looked at a small part of Freud's work, therefore it would be inappropriate to come to too many hard-and-fast conclusions. No one doubts the historical importance of Freud's work, but evaluations of its value to modern psychology vary from complete acceptance to complete rejection. Freud's ideas have won most favour in the world of therapy, where an understanding of unconscious desires, family relationships and dreams has proved invaluable to understanding what is going on in the minds of patients.

The major criticism levelled against Freud concerns the unscientific nature of his work. Freud, being a practising doctor and medical researcher, was trained in the methods of science. However, despite agonising over his scientific slackness (Jones, 1951), Freud rejected scientific psychology as simply too clumsy to tackle the issues he was interested in – how for example would you perform a laboratory experiment of the sort favoured by the behaviourists to see whether a dream represented wish-fulfilment? The result of Freud's rejection of scientific psychology is that many of his ideas are untestable. This is a source of great annoyance to psychologists, although as we have seen, some ideas such as reaction-formation have been successfully researched. A recent study by Harris and Campbell (1999) provides support for Freud's most fundamental assumption that we are influenced by unconscious processes.

KEY STUDY: K. Harris and E.A. Campbell (1999) The plans in unplanned pregnancy: secondary gain and the partnership. *British Journal of Medical Psychology* 72 (1), 105–120.

Aim: Unplanned pregnancy has always been of interest to psycho-dynamic psychologists, ever since Freud suggested that the motivation of women to have a baby was related to a wish to find a substitute for a lost penis (penis envy). Whilst psychodynamic psychology has moved away from ideas like penis envy, much interest remains in whether unconscious motives of some kind are a factor in some unplanned pregnancies. The aim of this study was to test whether women whose pregnancy was unplanned were more likely to have something to gain from pregnancy – and hence be motivated to become pregnant – than women whose pregnancies were planned.

Method: 128 participants were recruited from a North London general practice and a hospital. Participants were divided into groups of pregnancy status; planned-pregnancy, unplanned-pregnancy and a control group of non-pregnant women. In order to control for age, a matched design was used in which every woman in the unplanned-pregnancy condition was matched with a woman of the same age in the planned-pregnancy and control groups. Each group had a similar profile of social class, so it was unlikely that social class would affect the results. All participants were given a semi-structured interview, most in their own homes. The interview was designed to measure the *secondary gain* the women would derive from becoming pregnant. Secondary gain can be defined as the power of the pregnancy to have positive effects on the woman's relationships and life. Examples of secondary gains are improved relationships with partners and increased status in the family. An independent judge examined the interview transcripts and rated each participant for the likelihood of secondary gain they would derive from pregnancy.

Results: A strong association emerged between pregnancy status and secondary gain as measured by the interviews. Eighty-one per cent of the unplanned-pregnancy group were assessed as having some likelihood of secondary gain from becoming pregnant, 44 per cent having a high probability of secondary gain. By contrast only 16 per cent of the planned-pregnancy group and 8 per cent of the control group had a high probability of secondary gain. It was concluded that women with unplanned pregnancies were significantly more likely to be in situations where they stood to gain in some way from becoming pregnant.

Discussion

This study has important theoretical and practical implications, and has attracted some controversy. On a theoretical level, the results support the psychodynamic principle that our behaviour is affected by unconscious motives. On a practical level, this study might point towards ways of reducing unplanned pregnancy, for example identifying and challenging the common (and usually wrong) belief that pregnancy is likely to improve or save a poor or failing relationship. There have been challenges however to the usefulness of this study. One limitation is that researchers only interviewed women who chose to continue with unplanned pregnancies. Nothing was revealed about those who chose to terminate their unplanned pregnancy. The study has also been criticised for giving ammunition to politicians who claim that single mothers get pregnant in order to gain in terms of benefits and housing.

Winnicott's theories

To the layperson (and to psychologists not specifically interested in the psychodynamic approach) psychodynamic psychology is synonymous with the work of Freud. However, in reality there are a number of varied psychodynamic theories, linked by the basic psychodynamic assumptions discussed earlier in this chapter. For reasons of space, we cannot do justice to contemporary theory here, but we can look at one example of an influential post-Freudian theory, that of Donald Winnicott. Winnicott's work forms part of the **object relations school** of psychodynamic theory. Object relations theory is probably the most important influence on current psychodynamic practice. Like Freud, Winnicott wrote for many years on a variety of subjects, and here we can only briefly overview some of his more important ideas.

The unconscious mind

Winnicott's view of the unconscious mind differed from that of Freud. Winnicott (1958) believed that we are born as a chaotic bundle of emotions dominated by powerful instincts for intimacy, sociability and to form relationships with other people. If as an infant we succeed in building a relationship with our mother (or other caregiver), then we create from our chaotic emotions a sense of self or *ego*. If not we can become dominated by our unconscious mind, which Winnicott believed consists of *the sum of every time we were deprived of an emotional need as an infant*. Crucially, whereas Freud believed that we are all constantly influenced by our unconscious mind, Winnicott believed that if we develop a healthy ego, then we are only minimally influenced by our unconscious. Those who fail to develop a healthy ego remain governed by their unconscious sense of deprivation. The main factor determining whether we develop a healthy ego is the quality of our first relationship.

The first relationship

In Winnicott's theory, the first relationship is crucial for the healthy development of the child. The overriding factor in the development of the child's identity is the quality of mothering – i.e. how well the mother picks up and responds to the baby's needs. Winnicott called the mother who can adjust to the baby's needs the **good enough mother**. Winnicott (1988) described how mothers may naturally fall into a state of primary maternal preoccupation after the birth of a child. This is a temporary state in which she becomes focused exclusively on the infant and withdraws from other interests. The state of primary maternal preoccupation helps the mother understand and respond to the needs of the infant.

Winnicott (1965) suggested that if the mother fails to respond to the infant's needs and instead makes the infant fit in with her demands, healthy ego development does not occur and instead the child develops a **false self**. This is a kind of smokescreen behind which the child and later the adult hides because it has failed to develop a true sense of identity. The false self is dominated by a tendency for compliance as it has developed through serving the emotional needs of someone else and denying its own needs. The adult with a strong false self and weak ego continues to comply to the wishes of others and does not assert their own wishes.

In contrast to Freud, Winnicott played down the importance of the child's relationship with its father and emphasised the maternal relationship above all else. Winnicott was very much a traditionalist and saw fathers as providing materially for the family while the mother took care of the child's emotional development.

Evaluation of Winnicott's theories

In contrast to Freud, who based his ideas about child development largely on the recollections of adults, Winnicott tended to focus in his research on observable mother–infant interactions. Thus some aspects of his theory, such as the poor responsiveness of depressed mothers and the negative effects on children are testable and have been supported. Winnicott's most fundamental ideas – that infants seek out relationships and the fact that the mother–infant relationship is of critical importance for the child's well-being – are well-supported by research. Other aspects of his ideas such as the development of the false self are more speculative and difficult to test.

The major criticism of object relations theory in general and of Winnicott in particular is of their very traditional view of the family. Feminist writers have criticised the assumption that anything that goes wrong in the development of a child is the fault of the mother, and the implication that a woman's proper place is at home caring for her child. In the 1950s and 1960s when Winnicott did most of his writing, most families in Britain did consist of a working father and a full-time mother. This is no longer the case however, and children have proved rather more resilient to their mothers' working and the greater role played by fathers than we would expect if Winnicott's emphasis on mothering were justified.

Key application: mental health

The psychodynamic approach has contributed to our understanding of mental health issues by showing how experience and relationships in our early life can affect our later mental health. Thinking back to our case-study of Alex (p. 32), a psychodynamic approach to treating her panic attack would involve exploring the links between the symptom and her past. This is in contrast to a medical approach which would involve drugs to reduce her arousal levels, or a more mainstream psychological approach which would focus on altering the way Alex thought and behaved in the run-up to a panic attack.

Freud attempted to link specific mental disorders with specific unconscious events – for example, that anxiety-related conditions such as panic attacks are related to sexual frustration. Contemporary psychodynamic thinking has shifted away from these highly specific explanations and focused on two major areas, the general links between early experience and later vulnerability to mental disorder and the ways in which this understanding can be used therapeutically.

Early experience and later mental disorder

Central to psychodynamic psychology is the assumption that the child's developing personality is affected by parental relationships and trauma, and that later symptoms represent the fact that something has gone wrong with development. There is a large body of research linking susceptibility to mental disorder in adulthood to the experiences of individuals as children. For example, studies have shown that children who have suffered sexual abuse are more likely to suffer from a range of mental disorders in later childhood, adolescence or adulthood (Christo, 1997).

Depression appears to be particularly linked to early experience. Freud (1917) proposed that while some cases of depression were biological in origin others were linked to early experiences of loss. Research supports this idea. Bifulco *et al.* (1991) reported that depression was more common in women who had lost their mothers by death or family reordering (i.e. family break-up). Interestingly, death of the mother was more likely than loss by family reordering as an instigator of depression. In a large-scale study on patients suffering from depression, Kessler and Magee (1993) found that several childhood factors, including parental heavy drinking, domestic violence, the death of a parent and the lack of a close relationship with an adult, all increased the probability of suffering depression in adulthood. These studies clearly show that stress, traumatic experiences and lack of good relationships – we can collectively call these *psychodynamic factors* – increase the probability of later mental disorder.

Psychodynamic approaches to therapy

Psychodynamic therapies were the first psychological therapies, and they are still very popular with psychiatrists and other mental health professionals, although less so amongst psychologists. Because the psychodynamic approach sees psychological problems as rooted in childhood, it follows that those problems can be dealt with by exploring early experience, reliving traumatic experiences and gaining insight into how adult behaviour can be traced to early experience. A simple technique of psychodynamic therapies is free association, in which the patient talks of whatever comes into their mind. The rationale behind this is that whatever is really on the patient's mind will soon come up, and this will reveal unconscious anxieties and conflicts. The patient can then 'get it off their chest'; this is called catharsis. A fuller account of psychodynamic therapies can be found in Sue Cave's *Therapeutic Approaches in Psychology*, in this series.

Discussion of the psychodynamic approach to mental health

Of course these psychodynamic factors are not the only factors affecting mental health. There is, for example, an increasing body of

Figure 3.2 **Traditionally psychodynamic therapy takes place with the patient on a couch and the therapist sitting behind. Nowadays most psychodynamic therapists sit in a chair facing the patient**

evidence showing that genetic abnormalities are also linked to mental disorder. There may also be other psychological factors involved in mental disorder, such as the learning of abnormal behaviours. Most psychologists working in the field of mental health have an eclectic outlook and take account of a variety of factors that can impact on the mental health of the individual, including psychodynamic factors.

Psychodynamic therapies are exploratory and often – though not necessarily – long term, intensive and expensive. Burton and Davey (1996) have suggested that if psychodynamic methods are only as effective as quicker psychological treatments then they are a waste of money, and may even constitute an offence under the Trade Descriptions Act! However, it seems certain that, whilst psycho-dynamic therapies are not the first choice of treatment for everyone, they are the best approach for some people. Dare (1997) suggested that when the patient has a broad range of symptoms, a general dis-satisfaction with life and is motivated to explore the past, then they may be well-suited to a psychodynamic approach.

Contemporary issue: why do we love monsters?

Psychodynamic psychologists have always been interested in cultural trends in the belief that they reveal aspects of the unconscious mind. Of course, for a cultural practice to say something about the unconscious mind (which, according to the psychodynamic view is common to all humans), it must either be present across a large selection of cultures or have a clear equivalent present in a variety of cultures. Horror genres in the form of books and films are a fruitful area to look at from a psychodynamic perspective because, whilst not all cultures use the media of books or film, there are clear *equivalents* in the form of legends in a huge range of cultures. There are also instances of remarkable similarity between the legends of otherwise quite distinct cultures. For example, some form of 'undead' are to be found in the folklore of cultures as diverse as Haiti (zombies) to central Europe (vampires). From a psychodynamic perspective, the common idea of monstrous undead must serve a psychological purpose. They might for example represent an attempt to master the human fear of death. From a Freudian viewpoint, battling and overcoming monsters may represent the Oedipus complex, in which a monster – symbolising the same-sex parent – attacks but is vanquished (Minsky, 1998).

In a major study, Skal (1993) traced horror genres through the twentieth century, drawing associations between the monsters portrayed in horror and the predominant anxieties of the time. Following the First World War, a number of films such as *The Hunchback of Notre Dame* and *The Phantom of the Opera* featured disfigured heroes. According to Skal, these may have represented society's coming to terms with the mass-disfigurement resulting from the war. With the rise of Hitler and the Third Reich, wolves and werewolves became particularly popular monsters, symbolising the marauding, predatory nature of the Nazi threat. Skal draws special attention to the film *The Ghost of Frankenstein*, made in 1942, which, contrary to expectation, broke box-office records. A particular feature of the Second World War was the exchange of shells, resulting in huge areas of dismembered body-parts. Skal suggests that the figure of Frankenstein, who was constructed from dismembered body-parts, was a symbol of hope against the threat of dismemberment.

Following the war, with American and European politics dominated by the Cold War, film horror was correspondingly dominated by alien invasion, symbolic of the threat of war with Russia. Meanwhile horror comics became dominated by images of corpses returning for revenge on the living. Skal draws a link between this and society's collective guilt following the death of 40,000,000 people in the Second World War. *Godzilla*, produced in Japan in 1954, involved a radiation-mutated monster rampaging through Japan burning all in its path. Godzilla, with its elements of destruction and radiation, may have been a product of Japan's collective feelings about the atomic bombings of Hiroshima and Nagasaki.

In the late 1960s and throughout the 1970s, a major theme in horror was of horrific or demonic children. Examples included *Village of the Damned, The Omen* series, *Rosemary's Baby* and *It Lives*, Skal suggested that these films represented society's anxiety following the sexual revolution, and perhaps the horror following the revelation of the effects of Thalidomide, the anti-morning sickness drug that caused babies to be born with missing limbs. More recent trends in horror can also be linked to the anxieties of society. In the 1990s there have been a number of films involving computer domination – for example, *Terminator*.

Discussion

Skal has made compelling links between the prevalent anxieties in different historical periods and horror genres. From a psychodynamic perspective it is interesting that in all these genres, society's greatest fears at the time become personified by a monster which the hero or heroes battle and defeat. This symbolic battle is similar in function to the wish fulfilment proposed in Freud's dream theory. Tavris and Wade (1997) have compared the psychodynamic and social learning accounts of horror films. Social learning theorists are concerned that viewers might imitate violent or cruel behaviour portrayed in film. From a psychodynamic perspective, horror films serve a valuable purpose by giving us a way to deal with our fears.

What monsters frighten you now or did so when you were younger? Think about what these in particular might symbolise.

Contributions and limitations of the psychodynamic approach

There is no doubt that the psychodynamic approach has made a number of important contributions to psychology, including:

- recognition of the importance of the unconscious mind. Other branches of psychology have not effectively dealt with unconscious influences on our feelings and behaviour, yet, as we have seen in this chapter, unconscious influences are very important, especially in our more irrational behaviour.
- recognition of the importance of early experience and relationships. Few psychologists would deny that childhood trauma and family relationships have an impact on the developing child. The psychodynamic model is well-suited to understanding how and why these factors are so important.
- dealing with important and difficult questions. The issues addressed by psychodynamic psychology are of great importance to people. Questions like 'why did I dream that?, why can't I hold down relationships?, why do I have a problem with authority figures?, how on earth did I forget to go to that (dreaded) appointment with the bank manager?' are central to what the layperson wants from psychology, but hard to explain by other, more scientific approaches.
- a useful, though incomplete approach to understanding mental health. Although few psychologists believe that all mental health problems can be explained by psychodynamic factors, a psychodynamic perspective is useful in understanding how people's mental health can be affected by parenting style, early trauma, etc.
- a set of therapies and therapeutic techniques which can be of great benefit to those in psychological distress.

Of course, many psychologists – especially the more hard-nosed scientists among us – would argue that the limitations of psychodynamic psychology outweigh its usefulness. The following are some of the more serious limitations:

- theories are derived from case-studies. Grunbaum (1993) has argued that the idea of basing psychological theories on a small number of case-studies is not scientifically valid. This is particularly important when we consider that most of the cases on which psychodynamic theory is based are of people in distress, and are therefore not typical of the population as a whole. This has probably caused psychodynamic theorists to overemphasise the irrational nature of human behaviour.

- appealing but vague and untestable concepts. Whilst there is ample evidence for the broad psychodynamic principles like unconscious influences and the importance of early experience, the specifics of individual theories are another matter, and trying to perform research on ideas like the Oedipus complex has proved almost impossible. One of the major difficulties with the untestable nature of psychodynamic theories is that trainees have no way of knowing which of the available psychodynamic approaches to follow. People make choices to become a 'Freudian' or a follower of Winnicott without any reliable way of knowing who was right on the issues where Freud and Winnicott disagreed.

- psychodynamic reductionism. There has been a tendency in the past for those favouring a psychodynamic approach to try to explain *everything* by reference to psychodynamic principles. This has caused great harm to some people. For example in the 1950s and 1960s, psychiatrists, influenced by psychodynamic theory, blamed autism – a medical condition first apparent in childhood, characterised by difficulty in communication and repetitive patterns of behaviour – on poor parenting. More recently, Tavris and Wade (1997) have described the case of a psychiatrist who for 12 years failed to diagnose a case of myasthenia gravis, a treatable muscle-wasting disease, instead blaming the patient's repressed anger at her parents for her progressive loss of movement. This type of case illustrates the difficulties in taking a purely psychodynamic approach.

Summary

The psychodynamic approach to psychology focuses on the unconscious processes that affect our behaviour. The most famous psychodynamic theory is that of Freud. Freud is best-known for his 'structure' of personality, the ego-defences, his theory of psychosexual development and dream theory. Freud has been influential in therapy because his ideas are useful for understanding what is happening in the minds of patients, but he is less popular in academic psychology because his ideas are so difficult to test. Later psychodynamic theories differ substantially from that of Freud. Winnicott for example saw the development of the child as being rooted in its first relationship. The major application of psychodynamic psychology is in understanding and treating mental health problems. An interesting issue in psychodynamic psychology concerns our fascination with monsters, which may be seen as representing our unconscious fears.

Look back at the three vignettes in Chapter 1. Now that you know a little more about the psychodynamic approach, reflect on how well psychodynamic theory explains each of these scenarios. You may find it helpful to note down what aspects of each situation a psychodynamic approach can explain fully, and where it runs into some difficulties.

Review exercise

Further reading

Bateman, A. and Holmes, J. (1995) *Introduction to Psychoanalysis*, London: Routledge. A quite advanced but very clear account of the major theories and issues in psychoanalysis, including mental health issues.

Jacobs, M. (1992) *Sigmund Freud*, London: Sage. A detailed account of Freud's major ideas and discussion of the criticisms that have been levelled against him. This book deals particularly well with issues like the scientific status of Freud's work and feminist critiques.

Lemma-Wright, A. (1995) *Invitation to Psychodynamic Psychology*, London: Whurr. Aimed at the general reader as well as the psychology student, this is a very readable and balanced account of some of the major psychodynamic ideas.

4

Humanistic psychology

Key assumptions of the approach

Having read the previous two chapters on behavioural and psycho-dynamic approaches to psychology, you might well be asking yourself 'do we really need all these complicated theories to understand people?' If you are thinking something along those lines – and that is a perfectly respectable position for a psychologist to take – you may be more at home with the humanistic school. The fact that this chapter is the shortest in the book, whereas the chapter on psychodynamic psychology is the longest, reflects the fact that, in contrast to the psychodynamic approach which uses complex theories as tools to understand people, humanistic psychologists favour a few simple principles to understand people. You might also be wondering when the more positive aspects of human nature like creativity and kindness are going to crop up in psychology. These areas are the focus of the humanistic approach. Harkness (1998) has used the story of Percy the car to illustrate the principles of humanistic psychology. This is a shortened version of Percy's story.

Percy was born a small but unique car. He didn't have many parts but he did have a driving force, or 'engine' as other people called it. Percy soon realised that there were other cars and that they came in different sizes and colours. Percy decided that he wanted to be a red car. He would wave to other cars and some would talk to him. Some were friendly and admired his shape and colour. Others however ignored him or were horrible to him. The big cars always seemed to know more than Percy, and so he kept changing to fit in with what they wanted. One big car told Percy he was the wrong colour and Percy duly painted himself blue, although he felt sad about this. One day a fast car crashed into Percy and hurt him. Percy's view of the world had now changed, and when cars said nice things to him he did not believe them. One day Percy broke down. Fortunately he found a garage where he and a kind mechanic could thoroughly explore Percy together. Percy was there for some time and together they scraped off the blue paint. Percy was delighted to find his shiny red paint intact. He left and was a much happier car. He had learnt to value himself for what he was and no longer felt the need to keep up with faster cars.

Using the story of Percy we can pick out some of the important principles of humanistic psychology. The following are adapted from Lundin (1996) and Merry (1998):

- *People are motivated by the wish to grow and fulfil their potential.* We can see for example that Percy wished to become the best car that he could be, although it was not always clear to him what exactly that meant.
- *People can choose what they want to be, and know what is best for them.* Just as Percy chose to become a red car we can all make choices about how we wish to live. This emphasis on free will is in contrast to behavioural and psychodynamic approaches, which place more emphasis on what *makes* us behave as we do (this is called determinism).
- *We are influenced by how we feel about ourselves, which in turn results from how we are treated by others.* Thus, once Percy was

told he *should* be a blue car his self-perception changed and he ceased to like himself as a red car.

- *The aim of humanistic psychology is to help people choose what they want and help them fulfil their potential.* This means that humanistic practice, whether in therapy, education or in the workplace, is always centred around creating the conditions where people can make up their own minds and follow their own goals. Note that Percy's kind mechanic did not tell him that he should be red again, but explored him *with* Percy.

Humanistic psychology developed as a rebellion against what some psychologists saw as the limitations of behavioural and psycho-dynamic psychology. In the 1930s and 1940s the behaviourists were reducing all human behaviour to a series of conditioned responses and psychodynamic theorists were devising evermore complex theories of the unconscious mind. The humanistic movement aimed to restore balance in psychology by addressing human needs and ordinary human experience with a minimum of theory. The humanistic approach is thus often called the 'third force' in psychology, although it has less influence in contemporary psychology than that rather grand title suggests.

Now that you know a little about the ideas behind humanistic psychology we can go on to look at the work of two of its most important figures, Carl Rogers and Abraham Maslow. We can then look at person-centred counselling, the major practical application of humanistic psychology, and go on to examine the thorny issue of spirituality in psychology, a matter of much debate which is centred around the humanistic approach.

Rogers' theories

Carl Rogers was both a psychodynamically trained therapist and a behaviourally trained researcher. He was however not entirely comfortable with either approach, although he could draw from both (Thorne, 1992). Like Freud and Winnicott, Rogers' theories were *clinically derived* – i.e. based on what his patients said in therapy. Rogers' approach to what patients said was very different however. It is widely believed that Rogers' ideas may have been shaped particularly by one patient at the Rochester Society for the Prevention of Cruelty to Children. Rogers was seeing the mother of a delinquent boy for therapy, and, as he had been taught, making interpretations about her behaviour towards her son based on psychodynamic theory. The woman consistently rejected every interpretation and Rogers gave up. She then asked if Rogers took on adults for counselling. When he said that he did she told him clearly (for the first time) about her problems. Rogers was convinced by this incident that the aim of therapy should be to allow the patient (or client as humanistic psychologists call them) to talk freely and without any interference. Some of Rogers' clinically derived ideas are as follows:

The actualising tendency

Rogers (1959) believed that humans have one basic motive, that is the tendency to **actualise** – i.e. to fulfil one's potential and achieve the highest level of 'human-beingness' we can. Like a flower that will grow to its full potential if the conditions are right, but which is constrained by its environment, so people will flourish and reach their potential if their environment is good enough. However, unlike a flower, the potential of the individual human is unique, and we are meant to develop in different ways according to our personality. An unconscious **valuing process** guides us towards behaviours that will help us reach our potential. The valuing process can however be interfered with by too-strict social rules and by a poor self-concept. Rogers believed that people are inherently good and creative. They become destructive only when a poor self-concept or external constraints override the valuing process.

Development of the self-concept

Rogers noticed that in therapy clients would refer to themselves by saying, for example, 'I'm not being my real self' or 'I wonder who I really am'. Rogers began to place great importance on this use of the word 'I'. Remember that although Freud used the word 'I' or ego, he was far more interested in other aspects of the person. Rogers, by contrast, was interested in what people had to say about the ways in which they consciously saw themselves.

Rogers (1961) proposed that the most important aspect of the self-concept is **self-esteem**. Self-esteem may be defined as how much we like ourselves. Rogers believed that we hold in our mind an image of ourself as we are and an image of our ideal-self – i.e. what we would like to be. If the two images are *congruent* (i.e. the same) we will develop good self-esteem. The development of congruence and the resultant self-esteem is dependent on **unconditional positive regard** from others – in the form of acceptance, love and affection. Without a degree of unconditional positive regard we cannot self-actualise. Some children lack unconditional positive regard from others in childhood due to harsh, inattentive parenting or parenting characterised by conditional love – i.e. love which is only available if the child conforms to certain conditions. Such individuals are likely to have low self-esteem as adults, and are thus vulnerable to mental disorder, especially depression. The importance of self-esteem was demonstrated in a classic study by Coopersmith (1967).

KEY STUDY: S. Coopersmith (1967) *The Antecedents of Self-esteem*. San Francisco, Freeman.

Aim: Coopersmith was interested in the importance of self-esteem in child development. He aimed to learn about what effects having high or low self-esteem might have on a child and about what factors might determine a child's individual level of self-esteem.

Method: Coopersmith (1967) studied several hundred 9- to 10-year-old white, middle-class boys. He used four measures to establish the self-esteem of each boy. These were a psychometric test called the Self Esteem Inventory, teachers' estimates of how well the boys reacted to failure, a test called the Thematic Apperception Test (in which pictures are presented and participants say what they think is happening) and assessment of their confidence in an unfamiliar situation. On the basis of these measures, Coopersmith divided the boys into groups of high, middle and low self-esteem. He then looked at the characteristics of the boys in each group, including their confidence, ability to take criticism, popularity and academic success. Coopersmith also went on to investigate the types of upbringing the children had had, using questionnaires and in-depth interviews both with the boys and their mothers.

Results: Distinct differences emerged between the groups. High self-esteem boys were most expressive and active. They were the most successful and confident group, both academically and socially. The middle group were the most conforming. The low self-esteem children were the lowest achievers and tended to underrate themselves. They were the most socially isolated group, self-conscious and sensitive to criticism. Coopersmith found that parenting style was very significant. High self-esteem children had plenty of positive regard from parents, but they also had firm boundaries on acceptable behaviour. Low self-esteem appeared to follow harsh or unloving parenting or lack of behavioural restrictions. Coopersmith followed up the boys into adulthood and found that the high-esteem group remained more successful in terms of work and relationships.

Discussion

The Coopersmith study clearly supports Rogers' ideas – both that self-esteem is important for healthy psychological development and that positive regard from parents is a major factor in the development of self-esteem. However, Coopersmith also found that firm boundaries in behaviour laid down by parents predicted high self-esteem and this is perhaps more in keeping with behavioural and psychodynamic theories. Although Coopersmith's findings are widely accepted, he has been criticised on the choice of only white, middle-class boys as participants. We cannot assume from Coopersmith's study that different cultures create self-esteem in the same way, that girls develop self-esteem in the same ways as boys, or that the same factors are important in different socio-economic groups.

The fully functioning person

The mature or fully-functioning person has developed a high level of self-esteem through their exposure to unconditional positive regard, either in their upbringing or in therapy. Rogers (1959) identified five characteristics of what he called mature behaviour (p. 207). The first characteristic is *openness to experience*. This means that the person can accept and live with everything that happens to them, including both good and bad experiences, and not resort to ego-defence mechanisms. Rogers' second and closely related characteristic is *existential living*. By this he meant being able to live in and fully appreciate the present, not always looking back to the past or forward to the future. Rogers' third characteristic is *trust in oneself*. Remember how Percy, having been persuaded to paint himself blue, eventually came to trust his own choice of red, and was happier for it. Rogers believed that people's own decisions are the right ones and that we should trust ourselves to make the right choices. Rogers' fourth characteristic of the fully functioning person is *experiential freedom*. By this Rogers meant that we should be free of influences from our past, or 'emotional baggage', and be free to make whatever decisions we wish. Finally, Rogers identified the fully functioning person as having *creativity* – i.e. the ability to adjust to change and seek new experiences.

Discussion of Rogers' theory

Like Freud, Rogers has been so influential in so many ways that it is impossible to sum up his work in a couple of paragraphs. Perhaps Rogers' greatest contribution to psychology was to re-emphasise that the subject matter of psychology is the whole person, not just sets of processes like conditioning or the unconscious. Rogers also identified the study of the 'self' as what many laypersons needed from psychology. Rogers' methods of counselling (examined on pp. 69–71) have proved successful and extremely influential. Some aspects of Rogers' theories, such as the importance of self-esteem and the influence of positive regard on self-esteem, have been tested and are generally supported by psychologists. Other concepts, such as *congruence* and the *valuing process*, have proved untestable.

The severest critics of Rogers have been behaviourists like Skinner (see Chapter 2). Clearly from the standpoint of pure science, Rogers' ideas, derived (like Freud's) from patients in therapy, are subjective and rely both on the reliability of what patients said to Rogers and his interpretation of what he was told. Rogers' optimistic view of people as essentially good and striving to fulfil their potential has been seen as naive by psychologists from virtually all other theoretical backgrounds. Rogers has also prescribed how people *should* be – i.e. individual and striving in very culture-bound terms. Other cultures do not share the assumption that the highly individual person is the most fulfilled.

What do you think of the following ideas of Rogers?

1 That people are inherently good.
2 That fully functioning people accept change easily, therefore resisting change is a sign of not functioning fully.

Maslow's theories

Abraham Maslow was the second major figure in humanistic psychology. Unlike Rogers, Maslow was not a therapist. He began his career as a behaviourist but, upon the birth of his first daughter, rejected the idea that the mysteries of child development could be explained by simple processes of learning and, like Rogers, sought for explanations for the development of the whole person.

The hierarchy of needs

Maslow (1954) developed a theory of human motivation that aimed to explain all the types of human need and rank them in the order people seek to satisfy them. He distinguished between D-needs or *deficiency needs* which result from requirements for food, rest, safety, etc. and B-needs or *being-needs* which derive from our wish to fulfil our potential. We cannot strive towards our B-needs until our D-needs have been met. Maslow's hierarchy of needs is shown in Figure 4.1.

The idea behind the hierarchy of needs is that we ascend the hierarchy, satisfying each motive in turn. Our first priority is to satisfy our *physiological* needs such as for food and warmth, because we cannot live without these. Only when these needs have been satisfied do we seek out *safety*. Once we are safe, the next thing we need to worry about is our *social needs* – i.e. to belong to a group and have relationships with others. When our social needs are satisfied then *esteem needs* will become paramount. To satisfy our esteem needs, we need to achieve, to become competent and to be recognised as so. Once this has been achieved our focus will shift to satisfying our *intellectual needs*. Intellectual needs include gaining understanding and

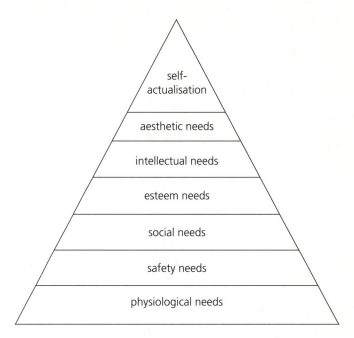

Figure 4.1 **Maslow's hierarchy of needs**

knowledge. Next in Maslow's hierarchy above intellectual needs come *aesthetic needs* – i.e. the need for beauty, order and balance. The final human need identified by Maslow is for *self-actualisation* – i.e. to find personal fulfilment and achieve one's potential.

The self-actualised person

Maslow (1970) described self-actualised people as those who were fulfilled and doing all they were capable of. By studying people he considered to be self-actualised (including American president Abraham Lincoln, physicist Albert Einstein and founder of psychology William James) Maslow identified 15 characteristics of self-actualised people. These are shown below:

1 Accurate perception of reality
2 Enjoyment of new experiences

3 Tendency to have peak experiences
4 Clear moral standards
5 Sense of humour
6 Feeling of kinship with all people
7 Close friendships
8 Democratic character accepting others
9 Need for privacy
10 Independence from culture and environment
11 Creativity
12 Spontaneity
13 Problem-centred rather than self-centred
14 Acceptance of human nature
15 Resistance to conformity

It is not necessary to display *all* these characteristics in order to be self-actualised, and of course it is not *only* self-actualised people that display them. Generally, however, those people Maslow considered to be self-actualised displayed rather more of these characteristics than the rest of us. Most of Maslow's 15 characteristics are fairly self-explanatory but you might be wondering what a **peak experience** is. Maslow defined peak experiences as moments when the world seems complete and one feels at one with it. Peak experiences stay with us and change our perception of the world for the better. For some people peak experiences are associated with religion, but they can also be triggered by art, music and sporting moments.

Maslow did not equate self-actualisation with perfection. Self-actualisers are merely fulfilling their own potential. Thus someone can be silly, wasteful, vain and impolite, and still self-actualise. Less than 1 per cent of people achieve self-actualisation because few of us satisfy all our lower needs on the hierarchy.

Evaluation of Maslow's theories

Maslow aimed for a psychology of human potential and achievement and in this he largely succeeded. His emphasis on the positive aspects of human nature is a good counterpoint to the behaviourists' emphasis on predicting and controlling human behaviour and the psychodynamic emphasis on all that can go wrong in human development. Maslow's ideas have also proved extremely useful in understanding human experience in a number of settings. For example Bentley (1994) has used the hierarchy of needs to help understand the experience of being homeless. Human needs as basic as food, shelter and safety are not reliably met in homeless people, and, as Bentley has pointed out, this explains why attempts to provide psychological help for homeless people have generally failed, unless the treatment is combined with housing.

Although Maslow's ideas are intuitively appealing and although they have been successfully used in a number of situations, there have been serious criticisms of his work. Maslow's research into self-actualised people was not carried out scientifically and the only criterion for identifying a self-actualised person was Maslow's own opinion. Like Rogers, Maslow has been accused of false optimism about human nature and largely ignoring the more negative aspects of human experience. Perhaps most importantly, as Engler (1999) has pointed out, Maslow's view of people as striving for personal achievement is extremely culture-bound, being firmly located in the individualistic culture of the USA. Cross-cultural research by Kitayama and Markus (1992) has shown that, whilst positive feelings in American students were associated with personal achievements, Japanese students by contrast tended to associate positive feelings with good relations with others. This shows that Maslow's idea of self-actualisation as individual achievement has limited usefulness in explaining the experience of people in cultures other than North America.

Key application: person-centred counselling

Humanistic therapies evolved in the USA in the 1950s. Rogers proposed that therapy could be simpler, warmer and more optimistic than that carried out by behavioural or psychodynamic psychologists. His approach of **person-centred counselling** has caught on in a big way, and in 1998 the British Association for Counselling reported that over half its members were humanistic in orientation, the next-largest group being psychodynamic.

Principles and techniques of person-centred counselling

One major difference between humanistic counsellors and other therapists is that they refer to those in therapy as 'clients', not 'patients'. This is because they see the therapist and client as equal partners rather than as an expert treating a patient. Like psychodynamic therapists, humanistic counsellors encourage clients to focus on and explore feelings, but they differ in being *completely* non-directive, refraining from asking clients to focus on or explain things they have said. A Rogerian would not offer interpretations but would merely encourage the client to keep on talking in the belief that they would eventually find their own answers.

One reason why Rogers rejected interpretation was that he believed that, although symptoms did arise from past experience, it was more useful for the client to focus on the present and future than on the past. Rogers followed a **fulfilment model**. Rather than just liberating clients from their past, as psychodynamic therapists aim to do, Rogerians hope to help their clients to achieve personal growth and eventually to self-actualise. Rogers (1961) suggested three core-conditions which would facilitate clients in their personal growth: **empathy**, **congruence** and **unconditional positive regard**.

Empathy is the ability to understand what the client is feeling. An important part of the task of the person-centred counsellor is to follow precisely what the client is feeling and to communicate to them that the therapist understands what they are feeling. *Congruence* is also called genuineness. This means that, unlike the psychodynamic therapist who generally maintains a 'blank screen' and reveals little of their own personality in therapy, the Rogerian is keen to allow the client to experience them as they really are. The final Rogerian core condition is *unconditional positive regard*. Rogers believed that for people to grow and fulfil their potential it is important that they are valued as themselves. The person-centred counsellor is thus careful to always maintain a positive attitude to the client, even when disgusted by the client's actions.

Because the person-centred counsellor places so much emphasis on genuineness and on being led by the client, they do not place the same emphasis on boundaries of time and technique as would a psycho-dynamic therapist. If they judged it appropriate, a person-centred counsellor might diverge considerably from orthodox counselling techniques.

As Mearns and Thorne (1988) point out, we cannot understand person-centred counselling by its techniques alone. The person-centred counsellor has a very positive and optimistic view of human nature.

The philosophy that people are essentially good, and that ultimately the individual knows what is right for them, is the essential ingredient of successful person-centred work. Mearns and Thorne sum up person-centred therapy as 'all about loving'.

Discussion of person-centred counselling

The common-sense ideas behind person-centred counselling are immensely appealing to many people, and this approach now dominates the counselling field. One reason for the popularity of the person-centred approach is its simplicity. Rogerian ideas are relatively easy to understand (though not to practise) so less academic study is needed for trainees. Like psychodynamic and behavioural therapies, person-centred counselling unquestionably works when applied appropriately. Greenberg *et al.* (1994) analysed the results of 37 smaller studies which looked at the effectiveness of person-centred therapy in a variety of situations and conditions. They concluded that overall person-centred counselling is as effective as other therapeutic approaches, and more successful than no treatment.

Person-centred counselling is best-suited to certain types of client. As in psychodynamic therapy, person-centred counselling works best for clients suffering a range of symptoms rather than highly specific ones. Greenberg *et al.* (1994) have suggested three factors that make someone suitable for this type of therapy. Clients must be interested in their inner experience. Someone who does not wish to talk about themselves in depth is not suitable for this type of therapy. Clients must also be highly socially skilled. Someone who cannot recognise the core conditions will not respond to them. Clients should further have a need for intimacy. Person-centred counselling involves an intimate relationship. Those who have a need for such a relationship may benefit most.

Contemporary issue: is there a place for spirituality in psychology?

The humanistic tradition in psychology is unique in that, with its emphases on personal development and the importance of how individuals experience the world, it is the only psychological approach compatible with the idea of **spirituality**. Although not all humanistic psychologists are religious or spiritual in outlook, and although you certainly do not have to be a religious or spiritual person to practise or benefit from humanistic psychology, there has been a close association between this approach and both the Christian Church and other religions such as Buddhism. Indeed one of the main factors in deciding what you think of humanistic psychology may be how comfortable you are with ideas like spirituality. No doubt to some of you spirituality will be an essential aspect of life, to others it will be meaningless. This makes defining spirituality extremely difficult. As Rowan (1990) has pointed out, by its very nature spirituality defies language. Thorne (1993) has attempted to express the concept thus:

> For me the individual's spirit or spiritual dimension is his or her creative source of energy which reflects the moving force within the universe itself. . . . I am not an isolated entity but rather a unique part of the whole created order.
>
> (Thorne, 1993, p. 74)

Rowan (1998) has identified three levels on which as psychologists we can discuss people. First, we can study people as things to be scientifically observed; second, we can think in terms of the way the human mind works; and third, we can view people in terms of their spiritual dimensions. Rowan has called the study of the spiritual aspects of people **transpersonal psychology** and defined its subject matter as 'the realms of the immutable, the infinite self, the absolute, open consciousness, bliss, unity with the divine, enlightenment and so forth' (Rowan, 1998, p. 578).

Discussion of spirituality in psychology

If we accept that psychology should seek to explain the aspects of human experience important to people then we have to deal in some way with ideas like spirituality. The difficulty comes when trying to study spirituality in anything approaching a scientific way. Terms like 'the infinite self' and 'contact with the divine', whilst very real and important to some individuals are so personal that arriving at a common definition and finding a means of measurement are nigh-on impossible. In a critical response to Rowan (1998), Hardman (1999) states that whilst the scientific study of people's spiritual experiences falls under the remit of psychology, ideas like 'infinite self' and 'unity with the divine' are the subject matter of theology and not psychology. The debate continues, and whilst the elusiveness of spirituality as a psychological concept will no doubt continue to plague psychologists interested in this aspect of human experience, the issue of spirituality is unlikely to ever disappear from psychology.

Consider your own attitude to spirituality. Do you see it primarily as an important aspect of human experience or a nuisance for the scientific study of psychology? Has this issue affected your own attitude to humanistic psychology?

Progress exercise

Contributions and limitations of the humanistic approach

- Humanistic psychology emerged in rebellion against behavioural and psychodynamic psychologies. It has remained a subversive movement rather than part of mainstream psychology, and humanistic criticisms of other psychological approaches remain as relevant today as when the movement began.
- Humanistic psychology reminds us that individual human experience is important, and that there are important aspects of human experience like self, peak experience and spirituality that are neglected by other approaches to psychology.
- Humanistic psychology has given us a simple, accessible and effective model of counselling. This has meant that many more people have access to psychological help than would probably be the case otherwise.
- Perhaps most importantly, humanistic psychology is alone in the major psychological approaches in emphasising the positive aspects of human nature and adopting a thoroughly positive attitude to humanity.

Despite these contributions, it is almost certain that humanistic psychology will remain a subversive element in psychology rather than part of mainstream psychology. Some of the major limitations of a humanistic approach are as follows:

- To an even greater extent than the psychodynamic approach, humanistic psychology has generated theories and ideas that have proved very difficult to test by scientific investigation.
- Because the subject matter of humanistic psychology is the experience of the individual person, there is a logical problem of applying theories generated from one individual to another. We cannot for example assume that two people experience the same thing when they speak of a peak or spiritual experience.
- Many humanistic ideas (particularly those around the development of the self) are extremely culture bound, and cannot easily be applied to a range of societies or historical periods.
- The humanistic emphasis on the individual person means that the importance of external influences on people's lives have probably been underestimated. As Lerman (1992) has pointed out, a battered wife can learn through humanistic psychology that she has a right not to be abused, but it does not in itself allow her to leave the situation safely.

Summary

Humanistic psychology emerged through the work of Rogers and Maslow, who sought to create a third force in psychology to escape the restrictions of behavioural and psychodynamic psychology. They proposed a simple and optimistic psychology with a minimum of theory that would address what people described as important experiences. The major application of humanistic psychology is in counselling, where the experience of the individual is of paramount importance. Although the humanistic perspective remains important, it has limited influence in psychological research because of its untestable ideas and emphasis on the experiences of the individual.

Look back at the three vignettes in Chapter 1. Now that you know a little more about the humanistic approach, reflect on how well a humanistic perspective explains each of these scenarios. You may find it helpful to note down what aspects of each situation a humanistic approach can explain fully and where it runs into difficulties.

Review exercise

Further reading

Merry, T. (1995) *Invitation to Person-centred Psychology*, London: Whurr. Designed for the lay-reader as well as the student, this is a readable outline to the nature and application of humanistic psychology.

Thorne, B. (1992) *Carl Rogers*, London: Sage. A thorough background to the life and theories of Carl Rogers. Covers the work of Rogers in more detail than is possible here.

5

Cognitive psychology

Key assumptions of the approach

Have you ever had the experience of looking for someone you know in a crowd and thinking you could see them, only to find that when they get closer the person you are looking at looks absolutely nothing like the one you are waiting for? Perhaps you have witnessed a crime and spent time looking through books of mugshots at the police station, only to get increasingly confused as you look at more and more pictures. You have probably at some time undergone the frustrating experience of trying in vain to recall something only to feel that it is on the tip of your tongue. What these experiences have in common is that they all happen because of the ways in which the human mind processes information. Cognitive psychology is the psychological approach which focuses on the ways in which we perceive, process, store and respond to information. The cognitive approach can be applied to just about every area of psychology, and later in this chapter we can have a look at a couple of examples of cognitive approaches. However, cognitive psychology is also a major field of study in its own right and it is to this that most of the current chapter is devoted.

It might be helpful at this point to spell out slightly more precisely what the subject-matter of cognitive psychology is. Broadly we can divide cognitive processes into five areas of study: perception, attention, memory, language and thinking. Perception refers to the taking in and analysing of information from the world. The processes of attention allow us to concentrate on one or more sources of information and to maintain this focus. Memory is the storage of information about facts, events and skills. Language involves the use of symbols as tools of both communication and thinking. Thinking is particularly difficult to define; however, Groome *et al*. (1999) have suggested that thinking involves 'a range of mental activities such as reflecting on ideas, having new ideas, theorising, arguing, making decisions and working out problems' (p. 166).

Let us now look briefly at an interesting study into one of the examples given above, the tip-of-the-tongue phenomenon. Many of us tend to scratch our heads or wave our hands around when trying to remember a word. Beattie and Coughlan (1999) investigated whether hand movements actually help people remember words on the tips of their tongues. Sixty students were divided into two groups. Those in the first group were told to keep their arms folded throughout the experiment, while those in the other group were allowed to gesture as they chose. Both groups were read 25 word definitions and asked to identify the words – this triggered the tip-of-the-tongue phenomenon. Interestingly the group with folded arms identified slightly more words correctly than did the group free to gesture, indicating that arm movements do not make it easier to remember words on the tip-of-the-tongue and may actually make it more difficult. Looking at the Beattie and Coughlan study, we can pull out some of the features of the cognitive approach to psychology:

- *Like behaviourists, cognitive psychologists see psychology as a pure science*. Note that the Beattie and Coughlan study was experimental (see Searle, 1999 in this series for a discussion of experimental methods) and carried out under carefully controlled laboratory conditions.

- *Whereas behaviourists are interested primarily in behaviour, and psychodynamic and humanistic psychologists are interested primarily in emotion, cognitive psychologists are primarily interested in thinking and related mental processes such as memory.* In the Beattie and Coughlan study, memory for words is being investigated.
- *The major influence on human behaviour is how the mind operates.* In the Beattie and Coughlan study, researchers were looking at whether there is a relationship between the mental processes of word recall and hand-waving behaviour.
- *Like a computer we are influenced by the ways in which our brains are 'hard-wired' and by the ways in which we have been 'programmed' by experience.*

The computer analogy

In the 1950s and 1960s cognitive psychology took over from behaviourism as the dominant force in psychology. One of the major reasons for this was the development of the computer. Initially the contribution of the computer to psychology was in giving psychologists a way of thinking about mental or *cognitive* processes. The use of the computer as a tool for thinking about how the human mind handles information is known as the **computer analogy**. By the end of the 1960s psychologists had taken the computer analogy to its next logical step and put together programmes called **computer simulations** that carried out simple cognitive processes such as storing information (see for example the work of Collins and Quillian, 1969, in Henderson, 1999).

By the 1990s the use of the computer analogy had entered a new stage where, with our increasing knowledge of the human brain, psychologists have been able deliberately to construct computers that work much more along the lines of the brain. This approach is known as **connectionist psychology**. A detailed explanation of connectionism is not within the scope of this book, but see Cohen *et al.* (1993) for a discussion. Cognitive psychologists vary considerably in how closely they believe in the computer analogy, but broadly we can say that cognitive psychology sees the human mind as operating somewhat like a computer.

Progress exercise

Think about the extent to which the human mind might actually operate like a computer. Consider all the ways in which the mind and a computer differ.

Strands of cognitive psychology

The cognitive approach to psychology differs slightly from the other approaches we have looked at so far in that it contains quite distinct strands, all of which share the basic cognitive assumptions but which use very different research methods. Groome *et al.* (1999) have identified three major strands to contemporary cognitive psychology. Experimental cognitive psychology uses experiments like the one we have already looked at by Beattie and Coughlan to explore how the human mind responds to different situations and hence how it works. Cognitive science is the branch that deals with constructing and testing computer simulations of human cognitive processes. Cognitive neuropsychology involves the study of cognitive processes in the living brain. This often involves the study of people who have suffered brain damage and so have lost or partially lost certain cognitive abilities.

Having overviewed the cognitive approach to psychology, we can spend most of this chapter looking at one area in depth, memory. We can look at the general nature of memory, theories of short- and long-term memory and how we might forget things. We can go on to look at eyewitness testimony, a major practical application of cognitive psychology and look at the current controversy over the reliability of childhood memories. We can also look at how cognitive principles can be applied to other areas of psychology.

Memory

Imagine for a moment what it would be like to live without any sort of memory. You wouldn't be able to speak because you wouldn't be able to remember words. You couldn't tie a shoelace because you wouldn't remember how. You would not know who your friends and family were. Your sense of identity would be limited as you wouldn't remember any details about yourself. Thinking would be tricky because you wouldn't be able to draw on past experiences. Nor would you be able to remember to do essential things like switch off the oven before your dinner burned. In short, you wouldn't be able to function as a human at all.

To show how disastrous it can be to lose even part of your memory function we can look at the case of HM (we use the initials to preserve HM's privacy). When he was 27 HM had brain surgery to relieve severe epilepsy. A part of his brain called the **hippocampus** was removed. This helped the epilepsy but severely impaired HM's memory. Although he can remember events prior to the operation almost normally he has been unable to form any new memories since. This condition is called **anterograde amnesia**. HM thus has to learn afresh everyday about his disability and the fact that his father has died. Although psychologist Brenda Milner has now been visiting HM for nearly thirty years – ever since the operation – he still does not know who she is. Although most aspects of HM's memory remained intact – he still has normal short-term memory, can recall most events prior to the operation and can learn new skills – he is severely disabled by his inability to form new memories.

Long- and short-term memory

Most psychologists make a distinction between short- and long-term memory. Short-term memory is where information that *we are currently concentrating on* is kept. As Eysenck (1998) puts it, short-term memory contains information in the psychological present. Long-term memory by contrast contains information in the psychological past – i.e. all the information that we have stored but are not currently thinking about.

Atkinson and Shiffrin (1968) produced an early model of short- and long-term memory. This is shown in Figure 5.1. In this model, information from the senses is stored very briefly in sense-organs, then passed on to short-term memory. From there some material is lost but some is passed on to long-term memory. When we remember something the information returns from long-term memory to short-term memory. Although most psychologists support the idea of

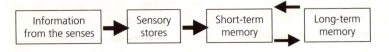

Figure 5.1 **Atkinson and Shiffrin's model of memory**

separate short- and long-term memory, we now have rather more elaborate theories of the nature of short-term and long-term memory. We can now look more closely at short-term memory, as represented by Baddeley's theory of working memory, and long-term memory, as represented by Tulving's theory of episodic and semantic memory.

Working memory

Baddeley (1986) has proposed an elaborated view of short-term memory called working memory. Strictly, the theory is not just one of short-term memory (Logie, 1999), because working memory constantly draws on knowledge in long-term memory. It does however focus on short-term memory processes. Working memory theory sees short-term memory as having three separate units: the phonological loop, the visuo-spatial sketchpad and the central executive. These are shown in Figure 5.2.

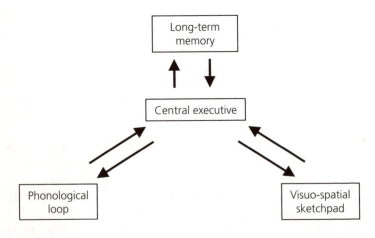

Figure 5.2 **Working memory**

The phonological loop holds words, and rehearses words that are currently being concentrated on. We can think of the phonological loop as an 'inner voice'. Baddeley *et al.* (1975) asked participants to recall short lists of words in order. They found that people could recall as many of the words as they could say in two seconds. Baddeley concluded that the phonological loop can hold two seconds' worth of words.

The visuo-spatial sketchpad functions as an 'inner eye'. Whenever we form a mental image of something we are thinking about we use the visuo-spatial sketchpad. As well as forming mental images Baddeley (1990) proposed that the visuo-spatial sketchpad is also involved in spatial tasks such as enabling us to find our way around and to judge distances. The central executive is the site of conscious thought. It is involved in planning and decision-making.

Baddeley's view of working memory is very different from the earlier short-term memory proposed by Atkinson and Shiffrin because not only is it a short-term store but also an active site of thinking, where new and old information can be sifted, sorted and combined and decisions reached. This process of deriving new knowledge by sorting and combining prior knowledge is called **mental discovery**. Mental discovery is one of the most important functions of working memory. Try the following exercise to demonstrate mental discovery (adapted from Logie, 1999). Imagine a triangle, a circle and an oblong. Now put them together. Draw the object you have created. You have now mentally created a new object, which may or may not resemble an object from your experience. This creative process is a simplified version of the way an artist or musician might plan the outline of a piece of art or music.

Outline the process of mental discovery you might go through in order to plan an evening out for a friend's birthday. Start by forming images of what you think the raw ingredients might be (these might include dancing, food, etc.). Now organise these elements into a plan for the ultimate night out.

Progress exercise

Evaluation of working memory

It is generally agreed that the idea of working memory is superior to the old idea of short-term memory as a simple short-term store of information. We can easily demonstrate that working memory is more than a short-term store by carrying out Logie's mental discovery exercise.

Many of the details of the working memory have strong supporting evidence. An experiment by Logie (1986) demonstrated that there are separate systems for handling words and images in short-term memory. Participants learned word-lists either by rehearsing the words or by mentally imaging them. They were then asked to recall the words while the experimenters showed them pictures. Those who had learned the words by rehearsing them (using the phonological loop) were unaffected by the pictures, but those using mental images (using the visuo-spatial sketchpad) were seriously affected by them. This clearly shows that the visuo-spatial sketchpad is a separate system from the phonological loop and that it is involved in both processing new and old visual information.

The principal weakness of working memory is the fact that although we know something about the phonological loop and visuo-spatial sketchpad we know very little about its most important aspect – the central executive. The central executive is a little like Freud's idea of the ego (see Chapter 3) in that although the idea is immensely appealing it is immensely difficult to investigate.

Episodic and semantic memory

Whilst working memory describes quite well our current beliefs about short-term memory, it fails to explore long-term memory in detail. Tulving (1972) contributed greatly to our understanding of long-term memory with his distinction between episodic and semantic memory. Episodic memory refers to our memory for events and semantic memory to our knowledge of facts.

Clearly if different parts of the brain are involved in memory of facts and events then this is powerful evidence that there are two separate systems of long-term memory. Tulving (1989) demonstrated that different parts of the brain are involved in episodic and semantic memory. Radioactive gold was injected into his own bloodstream and over 250 radiation detectors were positioned around his head so that where the radioactive blood travelled to in his brain could be seen. Tulving found that when he recalled events from his life the frontal regions of his brain became more active whereas when he recalled facts the back regions of his brain became more active. This certainly implies that there are different systems at work.

Although Tulving originally regarded episodic and semantic memory as two completely separate systems, in his more recent work (e.g. Tulving, 1987) he has explored the relationship between the two. One possibility is that semantic memories are derived from episodic memories. You can see, for example, that if you remember getting caught in the rain yesterday (an episodic memory) you will also know that it rained yesterday (a semantic memory). This means that facts are easier to remember if we can 'hang them on to' an experience such as a memorable book or lesson.

Evaluation of the episodic/semantic distinction

There is ample evidence from studies like that of Tulving (1989) that the distinction between memory for events and facts is a valid one. However, amnesic patients (who have lost part of their memory) do tend to have problems with both semantic and episodic memory – although the loss of episodic memory is usually more dramatic. This shows that the two systems are linked in some way.

While Tulving's distinction between episodic and semantic memory holds up (his early view that the two are not related does not), the episodic/semantic distinction does not explain the nature of long-term memory entirely. The study of amnesic patients has shown that there is a possibly more important distinction between implicit and explicit long-term memory. Explicit memories are those which we recall to consciousness in order to make use of them. Both episodic and semantic memories are explicit – when we recall a fact or event we are conscious of it. Implicit memories are those which allow us to do something (such as walk or talk) without thinking about it. Amnesic patients generally show impaired explicit memory but normal implicit memory – they can move and speak normally (unless of course there is another problem apart from the amnesia).

Forgetting

Forgetting is an everyday experience for all of us. Although we often think of forgetting as a pain – particularly if you have experienced it during psychology exams – in fact it is often useful. Think back to Tuesday three weeks ago. When you left the house what was the make and colour of the ninth car to pass you in the street? You almost certainly can't remember. This is not a bad thing! Without forgetting we would be plagued by irrelevant details of facts and events constantly intruding into our consciousness. We forget things for a number of reasons, both from short- and long-term memory. Here we shall consider two reasons why we might forget from long-term memory. Cue-dependency is a generally accepted phenomenon and probably the most common reason for forgetting things. Repression, by contrast, is much more controversial and probably occurs rather less frequently.

Cue-dependency

You may have had the experience of returning to a place, such as an old school or somewhere you lived, and had a flood of memories return. If you had been asked to recall these memories in a different environment you would probably have been hard-pressed to do it. This is because you needed the *cues* from the old place to remember. These cues could be visual but may also be sounds or smells. Cues need not even be in the outside environment. Sometimes we remember things if we return to the same mood or physiological state as we were in when we learned them. We can call this **state-dependency**, as opposed to **context-dependency** when we need cues from a place or situation in order to remember.

Cues are important in other situations as well. You can demonstrate the importance of cues for retrieving facts yourself by a simple exercise (based on Groome *et al.*, 1999). Winston Churchill and John Major are both twentieth-century British prime ministers. Common sense would predict that you should be able to remember more about John Major – he being the more recent of the two. However, the chances are that you actually remember Winston Churchill more clearly. This is because of the greater number of cues that we have to help remember him. Some of these are shown in Figure 5.3.

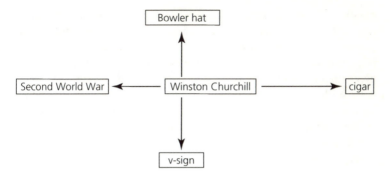

Figure 5.3 **Retrieval cues for Winston Churchill**

A number of studies have demonstrated the importance of cues in remembering. Godden and Baddeley (1975) gave deep-sea divers 40 words to learn either above or below water. They found that the divers who had learnt the words above-water remembered more words when above the surface and those who had learnt the words underwater remembered more when underwater again. Smells can provide powerful cues for memory. This was demonstrated by Aggleton and Waskett (1999).

KEY STUDY: J.P.Aggleton and L. Waskett (1999) The ability of odours to serve as state-dependent cues for real-world memories. Can Viking smells aid the recall of Viking experiences? *British Journal of Psychology* **90 (1), 1–8.**

Aim: The researchers aimed to test whether smells would act as cues for recall. Although previous studies had tested this idea in a laboratory setting the researchers wanted to see how effective smells were as cues in a real-life setting. They used a unique combination of smells present in a museum.

Method: 45 participants were selected on the basis of having visited the Jorvik Viking museum in York. The average time since their visit was 6.73 years. Participants were split into three groups. Each participant filled in the same questionnaire (alone) consisting of 20 questions about the contents of the Jorvik museum under two of three different possible conditions, with a 5-minute gap between each condition. In one condition, participants were asked to sniff a bottle emitting seven characteristic odours from the museum – burnt wood, apples, rubbish, beef, fish, rope and earth. In another condition the participants were given another bottle containing seven different smells not associated with the Jorvik museum. In the final condition there were no odours to smell. Group 1 had the Jorvik smells followed by the irrelevant odours. Group 2 had the irrelevant odours condition followed by the Jorvik smells. Group 3 had the no-smell condition followed by another no-smell condition.

Results: All the groups remembered more items on the second test than on the first. We would expect this as the participants had more time to think about the answers. However, as we would expect if the smells from the museum were helpful in aiding memory, the greatest improvement from the first questionnaire to the second was in Group 2 who began with irrelevant odours in the first test and then had the Jorvik odours in the second test. The mean number of the 20 questions correct for this group improved from 9.0 to 10.7. These results supported the idea that the odours from the museum provided cues which helped the participants recall details from their visit.

Discussion

This study clearly provides support for the idea that smells provide cues which help us recall information that we could not otherwise remember. The great strength of this study is that rather than setting up an artificial experiment in a laboratory the researchers used a real-life experience of the participants and tested them several years after the event. This means that the results can be applied to real-life situations. The technical term to describe how well a study can be applied to real-life is **ecological validity**. This study can be said to have good ecological validity.

We can use our imagination to help us find cues to assist in remembering things. Jerabek and Standing (1992) demonstrated that when participants were given material to learn then taken to a different room, they remembered more of the material if they were first asked to imagine the contents of the learning room. If you are a psychology student you are probably thinking by now of how you might use the idea of cue-dependence to help you remember material in an exam. Unfortunately you probably won't be able to take exams in the same room where you learnt the subject. However, it might be worth spending a little time in an exam recalling your classroom or lecture theatre and imagining the books and journals you read on the course. It follows that the more books and articles you read on a course the more potential cues you will have for remembering the material.

Repression

In Chapter 3 we looked at Freud's idea of ego-defences, including repression. As elsewhere the psychodynamic perspective emphasises the role emotional factors have to play in psychological functioning – in this case in memory. To recap briefly, repression takes place when we block memories of painful or shameful events or wishes from consciousness. This can take the form both of the complete blocking out of a memory so that we have no recollection of it at all, and of the general tendency to resist remembering unpleasant memories. Freud believed that repression was the most important ego-defence and that it was a common phenomenon, accounting for a substantial portion of all forgetting.

In Chapter 3 we looked at the type of evidence psychodynamic psychologists accept for the existence of repression. Cognitive psychologists, however, are a more cynical bunch and are generally very reluctant to accept case-studies and retrospective interviews as scientific evidence. This leaves us with something of a problem. The type of experiments that cognitive psychologists would accept as evidence for repression are difficult to set up because repression takes place – assuming it takes place at all – in unusual and traumatic circumstances.

There is another reason why cognitive psychologists have been slow to accept the idea of repression. Many instances of **recovered memory** – in which a traumatic event has been suddenly remembered after apparently having been forgotten – have turned out to be false. This can cause considerable harm and there are cases where adults have 'recovered' memories of sexual abuse apparently repressed during their childhood, and families have been wrecked, only for the memories to later turn out to be entirely false.

A new line of research into repression has been developed by Myers and Brewin (1994). People who have a tendency to use repression as a coping strategy can be identified by their scores on tests of anxiety and defensiveness. 'Repressors' score low for anxiety but, unlike truly non-anxious people, they score high on tests of defensiveness. Myers and Brewin identified female repressors and gave them and other groups, identified as low-anxiety and high-anxiety-highly-defensive, the task of recalling unhappy childhood memories as quickly as possible. The repressors took about twice as long to recall unhappy memories as the other groups. Researchers then set out to see whether the repressors had different childhood experiences – it might be simply that the repressors had fewer unhappy memories than the others. A semi-structured interview revealed that the childhoods of the repressors were characterised by very poor relationships with their fathers. This implies strongly that the reason why this group of women took longer to recall unhappy childhood memories was repression rather than a lack of unhappy memories.

The Myers and Brewin study is very significant because it is possibly the first successful demonstration of repression under laboratory conditions. As Eysenck (1998) has concluded, some forgetting is probably due to repression; most of the evidence, though, is still considered controversial. Cognitive psychologists have as yet no satisfactory way of knowing how common repression is or under what circumstances it occurs. Repression thus remains an important but frustrating concept in cognitive psychology.

Progress exercise

Where you do you stand in the debate surrounding repression? Do you think there is sufficient evidence for the existence of repression, and what do you think we should do when an important idea is so difficult to study?

Key application: eyewitness testimony

One of the ways in which cognitive psychology has been put to practical use is in better understanding and improving the accuracy of eyewitness testimony. Many criminal trials hinge on eyewitness accounts of crimes, and the testimony of eyewitnesses carries great weight with juries. However, human memory does not work like a videorecorder – when we remember an event we reconstruct it from all the information available to us, including our imagination and hints dropped by the questioner. In most everyday situations this tendency is harmless, but clearly it is a serious matter in the courtroom.

One line of research carried by Elizabeth Loftus and colleagues during the 1970s concerned the importance of the phrasing used when asking eyewitnesses questions. One of Loftus's best-known studies is examined in some detail below.

KEY STUDY: E.F. Loftus (1975) Leading questions and the eyewitness report. *Cognitive Psychology* 7, 560–572.

Aim: Loftus set out to establish whether participants could be persuaded by misleading questions to remember false details of a film. Specifically she wanted to see whether mentioning in passing an object not present in the film would influence participants to remember it later as present.

Method: 150 students were shown a short piece of film showing a white car that was involved in a crash. They then answered ten questions about the film. Nine of the questions were the same for all participants, but one question differed. Half the participants received the question 'How fast was the white car going when it passed the barn?' The remaining participants instead received the question 'How fast was the car going while travelling along the country road?' There was no barn in the film and the question mentioning a barn was meant to mislead the participants. One week later the participants returned and were given a further ten questions about the film, one of which was 'Did you see a barn?'

Results: As expected, the participants who had previously had the question 'How fast was the white car going when it passed the barn?' were much more likely to respond a week later by saying that they had seen the barn. Seventeen per cent of these reported seeing a barn as opposed to less than 3 per cent of the control group who had received the questions not mentioning a barn. These results indicated clearly that introducing something in questioning not actually witnessed can lead to its being remembered later.

Discussion

This study shows clearly how witnesses can be deliberately misled in questioning. It also casts doubt generally on the reliability of eyewitness testimony. Loftus and colleagues have carried out a number of related studies, and she is still probably the leading authority on eyewitness testimony. However, this and similar studies have their limitations. The study was carried out under laboratory conditions and the participants knew they were taking part in a psychology experiment. They were probably less physiologically aroused and less motivated to remember than they might have been in a real-life situation. This means that the study lacks ecological validity.

In another related study Loftus and Zanni (1975) found that participants were much more likely to report seeing a broken headlight if the questioner asked about *the* broken headlight as opposed to *a* broken headlight. This shows that questioners can use the definite article 'the' to mislead witnesses that something definitely happened as opposed to might have happened.

Some more recent studies based in real-life situations rather than the psychology laboratory have shown that eyewitness testimony may be rather more reliable than early studies indicated. Yuille and Cutshall (1986) carried out a study on 13 witnesses of a robbery in which a shopkeeper shot and killed the robber. Five months later they were questioned about the robbery and the researchers put in misleading questions like those used by Loftus, including the use of 'the' for events that did not occur. In contrast to the laboratory studies, Yuille and Cutshall found that the recall was very accurate and that misleading questions had no influence on the witnesses. Interestingly, however, five months may be a cut-off point for accurate testimony. Flin *et al.* (1992) compared the accuracy of eyewitness accounts after differing times had elapsed and found that accuracy declined sharply after five months. The effect was especially noticeable in children.

One aspect of eyewitness testimony where people are known to perform poorly is in face recognition. Studies (e.g. Bruce, 1982) have shown that faces are poorly recognised, particularly when details such as hairstyle have been changed or the person is dressed differently. In one recent study Hill and Bruce (1996) tested how well faces were recognised when shown from different angles and lit from different positions. Faces were presented in pairs to participants lit either shown from the same or different angles. Some pairs were lit from the same position and others from different positions. Participants had the task of saying which pairs of images were of the same person. It was found that when the faces were shown at the same angle and lit from the same position participants could match the faces correctly well over 90 per cent of the time. However, accuracy declined when the pairs of faces were shown from different angles or lit from different positions.

Because of the difficulty in recognising faces there has been considerable enthusiasm in recent years for using closed-circuit television (CCTV) to identify suspects. However, the picture quality of CCTV footage is often very poor and it seems likely that some false identifications are made. A study by Knight and Johnston (1997) showed that participants identified a greater number of people correctly on CCTV film when they saw moving images rather than stills taken from the film. This is probably because the participants were able to use additional information – e.g. the ways the 'suspects' gestured and walked, as well as their facial details.

Contemporary issue: the reliability of children's memories

A focus of much research in recent years has concerned how accurate memory is in children. Clearly the brains of young children are not fully developed and their cognitive functions may differ in many ways from those of adults. There are two major strands to research into children's memory: looking at how accurate adults' memory of their own childhood is, and looking at how reliable are children's accounts of things that have happened to them. For reasons of space we shall just look at the second of these.

The case of Kelly Michaels (reported in Tavris and Wade, 1997) shows how tricky getting information from children can be. Michaels was an American primary school teacher who was jailed for sexual abuse of children in her care. Four-year-old children made a number of allegations, including that Michaels had licked peanut butter from their genitals and inserted knives and forks into them. However, after she had served five years of a 47-year sentence Michaels' conviction was overturned on the grounds that the way the children were interviewed was likely to have led to false statements. A short excerpt from one such interview is shown below. The child has refused to repeat what they said in an earlier interview:

Child: 'I forgot.'
Detective: 'Now listen, you have to behave.'
Social worker: 'Do you want me to tell him to behave? Are you going to be a good boy, huh? While you were here did the detective show you his badge and his handcuffs? . . . Back to what happened with the spoon.'

Regardless of whatever was said in the previous interview, both the detective and the social worker are clearly putting undue pressure on the child to say what they want to hear. Children are particularly susceptible to this kind of pressure.

Ceci and Bruck (1993) reviewed over a hundred studies of the accuracy of children's memory for events they had seen or been involved in. They found that when questioned appropriately children could generally remember events very accurately. However, they also concluded that children were particularly *suggestible*. This means that, like the adults in Loftus's study, they could be influenced by questions to remember things that had not happened.

Ceci (1994) demonstrated how easily a child can be given a false memory. Adults repeatedly spoke to nursery school children about a man called Sam Stone who was very clumsy and frequently damaged things. Then 'Sam' visited the nursery. He did not damage anything, but when children were interviewed ten weeks later, using leading questions like 'I wonder whether Sam was wearing long pants or short pants when he ripped the book?', over 70 per cent of the children recalled that Sam had torn the book and 45 per cent reported having seen him do it!

It seems, then, that whilst children are initially capable of remembering events quite well they are especially vulnerable to distortion of their memories by leading questions and, like adults, they may lie or make up details to satisfy a questioner.

Applying the cognitive approach to the rest of psychology

So far in this chapter we have been looking at cognitive psychology proper – the study of cognitive processes in their own right. However, the cognitive approach has become influential as a way of thinking about other areas of psychology. Throughout psychology there are numerous examples of theories and models that make use of the ways in which we process information in different situations. We call these cognitive models. We can briefly look here at two examples of cognitive models: Beck's model of depression and Gilbert *et al.*'s model of attribution.

Some psychologists working in clinical psychology have found it very helpful to look at how people suffering from mental disorders process information differently from the rest of us. The best-known application of the cognitive approach to mental disorder is Aaron Beck's cognitive model of depression. Beck (1979) identified several cognitive symptoms of depression. Depressed people tend to have very negative views about themselves, the world and the future – Beck called this the cognitive triad. Depressed people also tend to attend to negative aspects of a situation and ignore the positive, and to jump to the most negative conclusions possible about a situation. Based on this approach to depression Beck developed a highly successful cognitive therapy. This aims to challenge and alter the faulty cognitive processes experienced in depression.

Cognitive approaches have also been applied to social psychology, for example in looking at **attribution**. **Social cognition** is the term given to the ways in which we process information in social situations. Attribution is an important aspect of social cognition, in which we make a judgement about why people behave as they do. Gilbert *et al.* (1988) have proposed a sequence of three cognitive processes that take place when we attribute a reason to behaviour. First, we categorise the behaviour (i.e. we decide what the person is doing). Second, we characterise the person on the basis of that behaviour. Third, we correct our judgement about the person based on information about the situation. Jarvis (1998) gave an example of this process in an everyday event, seeing a motorist at the roadside humbly apologising to a police officer. This is shown in Figure 5.4.

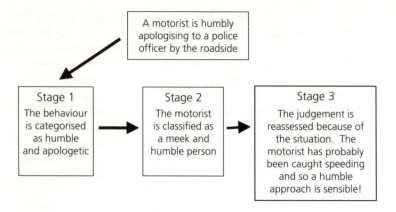

Figure 5.4 **An example of the attribution process**
Source: From Jarvis (1998)

Contributions and limitations of the cognitive approach

The cognitive approach has dominated psychology since its 'take-over' in the 1950s and 1960s. There are a number of strengths to the cognitive approach;

- Like behavioural psychology, the cognitive approach is scientific. Theories are testable and cognitive ideas are backed by a solid body of research. However, unlike the behaviourists, cognitive psychologists have found ingenious ways of investigating mental processes. Cognitive psychology has thus managed to give a good idea of the ways in which our behaviour is affected by mental processes.
- Cognitive principles have been successfully applied in order to understand many areas of psychology. We have looked at Beck's model of depression and Gilbert *et al.*'s model of attribution as examples.
- Cognitive psychology has numerous practical applications. Understanding eyewitness testimony and the reliability of children's memories are good examples of applied cognitive psychology.

There are, however, limitations to the cognitive approach to psychology and there are dangers in adopting a purely cognitive approach to psychology.

- Not all mental processes are easy to study using the methods of cognitive psychology, and there is a risk of important processes being ignored or discredited just because they are difficult to study scientifically. The classic example of this is repression, the existence of which was, until recently, denied by most cognitive psychologists despite numerous documented cases.
- It can be difficult to establish cause and effect when applying cognitive models to psychology. For example, Beck's model of depression sees faulty information-processing as the *cause* of depression. In fact the cognitive errors described by Beck are just as likely to be *symptoms* as causes.
- Some psychologists who adopt a purely cognitive approach can ignore other important psychological factors other than the ways we process information. This is called **cognitive reductionism**. An example of cognitive reductionism is sometimes seen in stress-management training in the workplace. A cognitive approach to stress management emphasises the ways we perceive things that are happening to us at work, and aims to help people view these events more positively. In practice, however, this kind of approach can mean that the importance of other factors like overwork and bullying are overlooked, causing harm to workers.

Summary

Cognitive psychology is a highly successful approach to psychology and has dominated psychology for some time. Its emphasis lies on mental processes and the ways in which they can affect our behaviour. Cognitive psychology is both an area of study in its own right and an approach to all areas of psychology. Memory is an important field of study in cognitive psychology proper. Much research has centred on the nature of short- and long-term memory and on how we forget information. A major practical application of memory research is in understanding eyewitness testimony. Important findings have included the importance of not asking leading questions in interviews, particularly of children. The cognitive approach has also been applied to other areas of psychology, including understanding depression and attribution.

Review exercise

Look back at the three vignettes in Chapter 1. Now that you know a little more about the behavioural approach, reflect on how well cognitive principles explain each of these scenarios. You may find it helpful to note down what aspects of each situation a cognitive approach can explain fully, and where it runs into difficulties.

Further reading

Baddeley, A. (1994) *Your Memory: A User's Guide*, London: Penguin. Written for the general reader as well as the psychology student, this is a very user-friendly guide to the major issues in memory.

Groome, D. *et al.* (1999) *Cognitive Psychology, Processes and Disorders*, Hove: Psychology Press. My personal favourite text on cognitive psychology. Very up-to-date and advanced but very user-friendly.

Henderson, J. (1999) *Memory and Forgetting*, London: Routledge. A comprehensive and very readable introduction to the study of memory.

6

Cognitive-developmental psychology

Key assumptions of the approach

Something for you to try if you haven't ever done it or seen it done. Next time you are talking to a child of six or under, ask them who makes the weather, and whether their toys have been behaving themselves.* The answers you get may tell you something interesting about the ways in which children's thinking differs from your own. You might find for example that the child firmly believes that the weather-presenter on television is personally responsible for the current weather. Trying to use logic to persuade the child they are wrong – for example by flicking channels and showing that there are several weather presenters predicting different weather for the following day – will probably cut very little ice. This phenomenon whereby children think that people are responsible for natural phenomena is called **artificialism**.

---

* Don't forget that the British Psychological Society code of ethics requires that you
must have parental permission to conduct any research on children.

Closely related to artificialism is **animism**, in which children think that inanimate objects such as their toys possess human attributes, including feelings and motives. In answer to a question about how their toys have been behaving, a child may respond that a teddy bear is presently in disgrace for deliberately refusing to obey instructions. Artificialism and animism were both first described by the eminent child psychologist Jean Piaget. Piaget developed the cognitive-developmental approach to psychology, and we shall spend a fair bit of this chapter looking at his work. First though, let us pick out some of the features of the cognitive-developmental approach:

- *The cognitive-developmental approach is primarily concerned with thinking and reasoning, as opposed to behaviour or feelings.*
- *Thinking and reasoning do not merely become more sophisticated with increasing experience, but the type of logic the child is capable of differs entirely according to its age.* Thus animism and artificialism are typical of the way in which a young child thinks about the world.
- *A major influence on human behaviour, feelings and thinking is the type of reasoning the person is capable of.* For example, if a child gets angry and punishes a toy, a cognitive-developmental explanation might focus on the child's tendency for animism. This is in contrast to a psychodynamic perspective that might emphasise instead the emotional significance of the child displacing anger on to a toy.

Later in this chapter we can look at how the cognitive-developmental approach has been applied to the field of education. First, however, let us look at two major theories of cognitive development: those of Jean Piaget and Lev Vygotsky.

Piaget's theory of cognitive development

Piaget researched and wrote on the subject of cognitive development from 1929 to 1980. Unlike previous psychologists, Piaget suggested that the way children think is not merely less sophisticated than adults, because it is based on less knowledge, but that it is also *qualitatively different* – i.e. children simply do not think in the same way as adults.

This idea was extremely radical when Piaget started out, but it has now become generally accepted in cognitive-developmental psychology. In fact you may regard this as common sense. Piaget was interested both in how children learnt and in how they thought. We can have a look at these issues.

How children learn

Piaget saw intellectual development as a process in which we construct an internal model of reality. In order to gain the information to construct this internal representation of the world we spend much of our childhood actively exploring ourselves and the outside world. You may have noticed that even very young children are inquisitive about their own abilities and about their surroundings. Piaget proposed that the child's mental world contains two types of structure, schemas and operations.

Schemas

Schemas are packets of information, each of which relates to one aspect of the world, including objects, actions and abstract concepts. Piaget believed that we are born with a few innate schemas which enable us to interact with others. During the first year of life we construct other schemas. An important early schema is the 'me-schema' which develops as the child realises during its first few months that it is a separate object from the surrounding world.

When a child's existing schemas are capable of explaining what it can perceive around it, it is said to be in a state of **equilibrium**. However, whenever the child meets a new situation that cannot be explained by its existing schemas it experiences the unpleasant sensation of **disequilibrium**. We are all instinctively driven to gain an understanding of the world and so escape disequilibrium. Piaget identified two processes by which equilibration takes place: **assimilation** and **accommodation**. Assimilation takes place when a new experience can be understood by altering an existing schema. For example, when an infant first crawls this new ability can be assimilated into the me-schema. Accommodation takes place when a new experience is so radically different that it cannot be assimilated into existing schemas and so a new schema needs to be formed. An example of accommodation occurs when the infant realises that its primary caregiver is a separate and independent person – leading to the formation of a 'mum-schema'.

Operations

As well as knowledge of aspects of the world we also need to understand the rules by which the world operates. Piaget called these rules **operations**. The reason that children think in different ways at different stages of their development is because their operations mature with age. Piaget believed that, while schemas develop with experience, operations develop as the child's brain matures. The very young child does not have operations at all. The first operations to appear are concrete – i.e. children can understand the rules governing something only if they can see it. Later, rules governing abstract concepts can be understood. The errors of logic that Piaget identified in children's thinking take place because of the limited operations available to them. Piaget's stage theory of development (see pp. 105–106) is based around the maturing of operations.

How children think

Piaget conducted a series of studies of children's mental abilities. Piaget's first studies were observations of children playing and attempting to solve problems. He noted that different children of the same age tended to make the same mistakes, and that these mistakes seemed to be based on the same faulty logic. From these observations was born the idea that children do not just know less but think *differently* from adults. Piaget later developed the use of clinical interviews to confirm the idea that children's logic is different to that of adults. When children made mistakes in the task they were attempting to carry out, Piaget asked them questions about how they had come to their conclusions. This allowed him to see what logical errors children were making.

Piaget identified certain logical errors as typical of children of different ages. Piaget saw different stages of cognitive development as being characterised by different types of logical error. These errors included animism and artificialism, which we have already discussed, and object impermanence, egocentrism and failure to conserve.

Object impermanence

This error was believed by Piaget to occur in children under about 8 months. Piaget (1963) noticed that young infants would ignore even highly attractive objects if they were removed from sight. Piaget took this to mean that very young children were unaware of the continued existence of objects once they were out of sight. Clearly when a child grasps the fact that physical objects continue to exist when not in the field of vision they have made a leap in their understanding of the world.

Egocentrism

This refers to children's tendency to see the world entirely from their own perspective, and to have great difficulty in seeing the world from the viewpoint of others. Unlike object impermanence and animism, which are associated with specific ages, egocentrism declines gradually throughout childhood. Piaget saw egocentrism as applying to both abstract and concrete concepts. Thus as a girl of 4 years you might be expected to understand the idea that you have a brother. However, you would probably have some difficulty with the idea that your brother had a sister (Flanagan, 1996). A classic study by Piaget and Inhelder (1956) illustrated egocentrism in the physical environment.

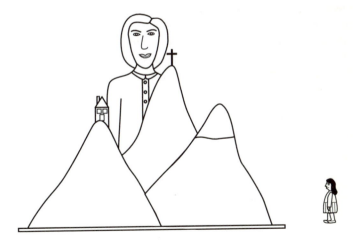

Figure 6.1 **The three mountains task**
Source: After Piaget and Inhelder (1952)

In the three mountains experiment (see Figure 6.1) each papier mâché mountain had a different marker on the top. A doll was placed to the side of the three mountains. Children were shown pictures of the scene from different viewpoints and they had to select the picture that best matched what the doll could 'see'. Piaget and Inhelder found that children under 7 years had difficulty with this task and tended to choose the picture of the scene from their own point of view. Egocentrism also occurs in more abstract thinking, for example in the child's conception of morality. **Moral realism** is the state where the child can only see right and wrong from one point of view at a time. Using his clinical interview method, Piaget found that children could not take into account the motives of others because they could not conceive of the situation from their point of view. Children therefore tend to make very sharp and one-sided judgements on moral decisions.

Failure to conserve

Piaget (1952) found that young children have difficulty with the idea of **conservation** – i.e. that things can remain the same in quantity despite changes in their appearance. Piaget demonstrated this in a number of situations, two of which are particularly well known. In number conservation tasks (see Figure 6.2), Piaget found that if two rows of counters are laid out side by side, with the same number of counters spaced apart at the same distance children correctly spotted that there were the same number of counters in each row. If however the counters in one of the rows were pushed together, young children typically thought that there were now fewer counters in that row.

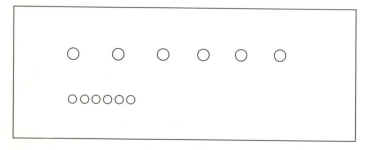

Figure 6.2 **Number conservation**

A related ability is liquid conservation. Piaget found that if children see two beakers side by side with liquid coming up to the same height in each they can correctly spot the fact that they contain the same amount of liquid. If, however, liquid is poured from one of the beakers into a tall thin container, young children typically said that there was now more liquid in the taller container (see Figure 6.3).

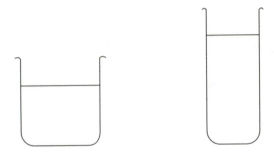

Figure 6.3 **Liquid conservation**

Piaget's stage theory

Based on the types of logical errors children made at different ages, Piaget (1972) proposed a stage theory of development in which there were four distinct stages:

- sensorimotor stage: 0–2 years;
- preoperational stage: 2–7 years;
- concrete operational stage: 7–11 years;
- formal operational stage: 11 years+.

Piaget believed that we all pass through all four stages, although we may vary in the age at which we achieve each stage. We reach each stage when our brain is mature enough to permit the use of new types of logic or *operations*. Let us look briefly at the type of thinking that takes place at each stage.

Sensorimotor stage

In our first two years Piaget believed that our main focus is on physical sensation and on learning to coordinate our own bodies. We learn that certain actions have specific effects. Thus babies are fascinated when they realise that they can move parts of their body and, later, other objects. By the second year of life infants will deliberately experiment with actions to discover their effects. By about 9 months infants begin to understand object permanence. By the end of the sensorimotor stage infants are aware of themselves as separate from the rest of the world and have begun to develop language.

Preoperational stage

The child's thinking is now based around symbolic thought using language rather than physical sensation. However, the child has little grasp of logical rules (hence *preoperational*) and deals with the world very much as it appears rather than as it is. For example, preoperational children are highly egocentric, have difficulty in conservation, and tend to believe in animism and artificialism.

Concrete operational stage

The child is now mature enough to use logical thought or operations but children can only apply logic to present and physical objects (hence *concrete* operational). Thus children now lose their tendency for animism and artificialism. They become less egocentric and better at conservation tasks. However, concrete operational children have great difficulty carrying out logical tasks without the physical objects in front of them. Smith *et al.* (1998) have given an example. Children given three dolls (Edith, Susan and Lily) with different hair colours have no difficulty in identifying which doll has the darkest hair. However, concrete operational children when asked the question 'Edith is fairer than Susan. Edith is darker than Lily. Who is the darkest?' have great difficulty because they cannot reason with symbols alone.

Formal operational stage

In the formal operational stage children become capable of following the form of an argument and not being distracted by content (hence *formal* operations). Phillips (1975) illustrated the difference between concrete and formal operational thinking by giving children syllogisms; for example:

'All children like spinach;
boys are children;
therefore boys like spinach.'

Formal operational thinkers responded to the *form* of the syllogism and reacted to the logic in the three statements. Concrete operational thinkers, however, were distracted by their own opinions of spinach.

Inhelder and Piaget (1958) gave children of secondary school age a selection of scientific experiments. The task was to make up hypotheses and test them. Although the children were given equipment to carry out the tasks, abstract reasoning was required to predict the results. The researchers found that between the ages of 11 and 15 children could successfully do this. Piaget took this to mean that children had entered a new stage of adult logic, where abstract reasoning was possible. As well as systematic abstract reasoning, formal operations permits the development of a system of values and ideals, and an appreciation of philosophical issues.

What does your experience tell you about formal operational thinking. If you are a psychology student you can probably perform formal operational tasks because abstract reasoning is necessary to understand psychological theory, but do you agree with Piaget that all or most people can think this way?

Progress exercise

Later research on Piaget's ideas

Most psychologists are quite accepting of Piaget's general principles that children's thinking is fundamentally different from that of adults, and that the type of logic of which we are capable changes with age. However, some researchers have quibbled with the details of Piaget's findings, particularly with regard to the ages at which children become capable of specific tasks. In one classic study, McGarrigle and Donaldson (1974) suggested that children understand conservation rather earlier than Piaget believed.

KEY STUDY: J. McGarrigle and M. Donaldson (1974) Conservation accidents. *Cognition* 3, 341–350.

Aim: McGarrigle and Donaldson (1974) set out to discover whether children could understand conservation of number at an earlier age than had been suggested by Piaget. They proposed that in the classic Piaget (1952) experiment, children estimated there to be fewer counters when they were pushed closer together *because the experimenter had obviously deliberately moved them*. They aimed to see whether children conserved better if they thought the counters had been moved accidentally.

Method: 80 children aged between 4 and 6 years took part in two conditions. In one condition they performed the original Piagetian procedure, in which children were shown two lines of counters containing the same number of counters the same distance apart. The researcher moved one line of counters closer together and children had to estimate whether there were now the same number. In the second condition, instead of the experimenter 'naughty teddy' appeared and mischievously moved one row of counters together. The child was asked to return naughty teddy to his box, then asked whether the two rows of counters contained the same number. All children took part in both conditions. Counterbalancing was used to prevent order effects – i.e. half the children encountered the naughty teddy condition first and half the Piagetian condition first.

Results: In the standard Piagetian condition 13 of the 80 children successfully realised that there were the same number of counters in the shorter row, while in the naughty teddy condition 50 of the children successfully conserved. This suggests that McGarrigle and Donaldson were correct in suggesting that young children can successfully conserve when not put off by the fact that an adult has deliberately altered the appearance of one of the rows.

Discussion

This is a cleverly designed study which clearly supports the idea that children understand conservation at an earlier age than that suggested by Piaget. However, not all attempts to replicate the study have produced the same results. We are therefore unsure at what age children begin to successfully conserve number.

Other studies have challenged the idea that children do not achieve object permanence until they are over 6 months old. Baillargeon and DeVos (1991) devised an experiment in which infants watched a toy disappear behind a screen in the upper half of which was a window. The toy was either tall, in which case it could be watched as it passed the window, or short, in which case it passed beneath the window. When an 'impossible' condition was created in which a tall object moved behind the screen but failed to appear at the window, young babies showed particular interest in the object when it emerged from the screen. This suggested that they understood the principle of object permanence well enough to know that the tall object should have been visible.

More recently Bradmetz (1999) tested Piaget's idea that the majority of children achieve formal operations in late childhood: 104 children were followed up until they were 18 years old, and tested on a variety of formal operational tasks based on those used by Piaget himself, including hypothesis testing. The majority of the children did not achieve formal operations. This, taken along with the studies of McGarrigle and Donaldson and Baillargeon and DeVos, suggests that Piaget underestimated the abilities of younger children and overestimated the abilities of older children.

Vygotsky's theory of cognitive development

Vygotsky was a contemporary of Piaget, writing in the Soviet Union during the 1920s and 1930s. His work was not published in the Western world, however, until the 1960s, since which time it has grown hugely in influence. Vygotsky was an admirer of Piaget's and while he agreed with Piaget that cognitive development takes place in stages characterised by different styles of thinking, he disagreed with Piaget's view of the child as exploring the world alone and forming its own internal representation of reality.

The social and cultural basis of learning

Whereas Piaget saw children as learning by individual discovery, Vygotsky placed more emphasis on the role played by adults and other children in facilitating the child's development. According to Vygotsky children are born with relatively basic mental functions such as the ability to perceive the outside world and to focus their attention. However, children lack higher mental functions such as memory, thinking and problem-solving. These higher mental functions are seen as 'tools' of the culture in which the individual lives and they are cultural in origin. Tools are transmitted to children by older members of the culture during guided learning experiences. Experiences with other people gradually become internalised and form the child's internal representation of the world. Thus the way each child thinks is shared with other members of its culture.

The zone of proximal development

Vygotsky believed that although children would eventually learn some concepts on their own during everyday experience they could develop far more during interaction with others. Children could never develop formal operational thinking without the help of others. Vygotsky called the difference between what a child can learn on its own and what it could potentially learn through interaction with others the zone of proximal development (ZPD). Whereas Piaget believed that the limiting factor in what a child could learn at any time was its stage of development, Vygotsky believed that the crucial factor was the availability of other 'experts' who could instruct the child. Unlike Piaget Vygotsky emphasised instruction from others in how to do things in order for the child to achieve its potential. As the child progresses through a zone of proximal development, or learning cycle, the amount of instruction will reduce. At first explicit and detailed instructions are needed, but later on hints and prompts are all that are needed to help the child progress.

The role of language

Vygotsky placed far more emphasis on language in cognitive development than did Piaget. For Piaget language appeared when the child had reached a sufficiently advanced stage of development. The sophistication of the child's language was seen as dependent on its current level of cognitive development. For Vygotsky, however, language developed from social interactions with others. At first the sole function of language is communication, and language and thought develop separately, but later the child internalises language and learns to use it as a tool to aid problem-solving. In the preoperational stage, as children learn to use language to solve problems, they speak aloud while solving problems (you can hear children doing this yourself). Once in the concrete operational stage this inner speech becomes silent.

Discussion of Vygotsky

In the next section, which deals with the ways in which the ideas of Piaget and Vygotsky have been applied to education, we will see that there is evidence to support the idea that children learn better from other people than they do by discovery learning. This supports Vygotsky's ideas about how children learn as opposed to those of Piaget. This still leaves us with the question of children's motivation to learn. Remember that Piaget emphasised that children were born with an instinct to find out about the world. Trevarthen (1995) has addressed this by suggesting that what children are actually born with is a need to impose *meaning* on their world. This can be achieved by individual discovery but is more easily and completely achieved when the child can take on the beliefs, understanding and knowledge of their culture.

Key application: applying psychology to teaching

Think about how you have been taught in primary and secondary school and at college. You will probably have experienced a variety of teaching styles. The teaching and learning styles we employ nowadays in schools and colleges have been profoundly influenced by cognitive-developmental psychology. Shortly, we will look at how both Piaget's and Vygotsky's ideas have influenced teaching. First, though, it is worth taking a brief look at the historical background of the application of cognitive-developmental theory to education.

Historical background

Prior to the 1960s teaching methods in Britain were primarily influenced by behaviourist psychology (see Chapter 2). The behaviourists favoured a transmission model of education (Faulkner, 1995). This involves giving children a range of knowledge and skills by direct instruction. Direct instruction means a teacher delivering material to children by talking and by writing or dictating notes (this is often called **didactic** or chalk-and-talk teaching). Children were seen as passive receivers of knowledge. This fitted in well with the then-popular behaviourist view of children. There was little effort made to tailor what children were taught to what they were capable of understanding. This is perfectly acceptable within a behaviourist framework because behaviourists do not agree with the idea of developmental stages – a child's intellectual development is simply measured by how much it knows.

However, by the 1960s the work of Piaget and Vygotsky was becoming very influential in both psychology and education, and other progressive or **child-centred** models of learning began to appear. The child-centred tradition challenged the idea that children should be taught didactically. This view became increasingly popular following the Plowden report.

The Plowden Report

The Plowden committee was set up to examine ways of improving primary education. The committee's report, published in 1967, recommended a shift away from didactic teaching towards child-centred teaching. We can pick out three main messages from the Plowden Report. Children need to be given individual attention and cannot all be treated the same way. They should not be taught things until they are developed enough intellectually to cope with them. Children mature intellectually, physically and emotionally at different rates.

Teachers need to cater for the individual needs of children; in practice this means allowing children to learn at their own pace and this cannot be achieved by direct instruction. As you may have spotted, this has a strong Piagetian flavour, and in fact the authors of the Plowden Report were greatly influenced by Piaget's theories.

Implications of Piagetian theory for teaching style

Piaget did not focus in his writing on education, regarding it as best left to teachers. However, following the Plowden Report teachers enthusiastically put Piagetian principles into practice in the classroom. The following are some of the main implications of Piagetian theory for classroom practice.

1   As children think differently and less logically than adults, teachers should make an effort to adapt to the way children think rather than expect children to adapt to them. One way in which this can be achieved is for the teacher to create situations where the child can learn for his or herself rather than rely on simply telling children facts. This leads us to the next Piagetian principle.

2   Children learn best by *discovery*. The role of the teacher is thus to set up tasks in which children can work things out for themselves. In effective child-centred learning the teacher does not leave children to their own learning but presents children with well-thought-out tasks specifically designed to lead them to discover and work things out for themselves. A variety of tasks need to be given, helping the child construct knowledge of the world. In the nursery and primary school, materials like water, sand, bricks and crayons all help children build constructions (external and internal). Later, projects and science practicals help children explore the nature of their world.

3   The aim of education is to develop children's thinking. This means that when children try to work things out, what is important is their reasoning rather than the answer. It is therefore very important that teachers do not penalise children for answers that are wrong but well-reasoned. Instead the task of the teacher is to tease out *how* the child came to the wrong conclusion and encourage them in further thinking.

Implications of Vygotsky's theory for teaching style

Unlike Piaget, Vygotsky was interested in applying his ideas directly to education. We can consider the work of Vygotsky together with that of a contemporary cognitive-developmental psychologist, Jerome Bruner. Bruner had similar ideas to those of Vygotsky, but developed them rather further in relation to education. Bruner has, for example, looked at **scaffolding**, the process by which adults guide children through their zone of proximal development. Smith *et al.* (1998) describe the implications of Vygotsky's and Bruner's work for teaching.

1 Although Vygotsky and Bruner have proposed a more important role for adults in children's learning than did Piaget, they did not favour a wholesale return to didactic teaching. Instead they proposed that while children should still be engaged in active learning, the teacher should actively assist children in what they are doing. In theoretical terms this means that children are working within their zone of proximal development and teachers are providing the scaffolding for children to move through the ZPD. Shortly, we can look a little closer at the idea of scaffolding.

2 Vygotsky in particular has proposed that, in addition to teachers, peers are important influences on children's cognitive development. Cooperative groupwork as opposed to individual discovery learning appears to speed up children's development. Bennett and Dunn (1992) investigated the effects of cooperative group work (CGW) on the development of primary school children. They found that children who worked in cooperative work groups showed more advanced thinking and better language than those who worked alone.

3 An extension of the idea of cooperative groupwork is peer tutoring, where one child instructs another who is slightly less advanced. Foot *et al.* (1990) explain the success of peer tutoring using Vygotsky's theory. One child can be effective in guiding another through the ZPD because, having only recently made that advance themselves, they are in a good position to see the difficulties faced by the other child and provide appropriate scaffolding.

Now let us return to look in a little more detail at scaffolding. A classic study by Wood *et al.* (1976) looked at the ways in which teachers scaffold children's learning.

KEY STUDY: D.J. Wood, J.S. Bruner and G. Ross (1976) The role of tutoring in problem-solving. *Journal of Child Psychology and Psychiatry* 17, 89–100.

Aim: The researchers were not seeking to test a specific hypothesis. Instead the aim of the study was to see how teachers scaffolded children's learning as they tried to solve the problem of building a three-dimensional structure.

Method: 30 children took part in the study. There were ten 3-year-olds, ten 4-year-olds and ten 5-year-olds. Each age group contained equal numbers of girls and boys. The researchers had designed a task for the children. They had to construct a six-level wooden pyramid out of 21 wooden blocks, one base and four blocks of each size to make up the five layers. The same tutor was observed with children from each age group. Each child undertook the task separately. Each child was allowed a period of free play with the blocks, then the tutor showed them how to join two blocks together. Three types of tutor intervention were classified by the observers, depending on the child's success. If the child did not join blocks together the tutor *directly intervened* by joining them herself. If the child tried to join blocks together but failed, the tutor *verbally corrected* them. If the child succeeded in joining blocks but could not work out how to build the whole structure, the tutor would *verbally direct* them to go on to the next stage.

Results: The number of direct interventions, verbal corrections and verbal directions were recorded for each child and the median for each age group calculated. These are shown in the table below:

Age	Direct interventions	Verbal corrections	Verbal directions
3 years	12.0	3.0	5.0
4 years	6.0	5.0	8.0
5 years	3.0	4.5	3.0

Overall 5-year-olds received significantly less help. You can also see that 3-year-old children received more direct intervention. The interventions used with 4- and 5-year-olds were significantly more likely to be verbal.

Discussion

From these results the researchers concluded that the tutor was scaffolding children's learning in much the ways that would be predicted by Bruner's theory. More direct intervention was used where children were near the start of the ZPD and more prompts and corrections as children neared the end of the ZPD and were largely self-directing.

Contemporary issue: computer-aided learning

In the 1990s more and more of us, including children, are using computers in a variety of contexts and for a variety of tasks. Littleton (1995) suggested that the use of computers in learning may provide opportunities for helping children learn more quickly, to learn in different ways, to make children more confident and to motivate disaffected children. On the other hand the use of computers may raise issues of socially isolating learners, losing something from the teacher–learner relationship, excessive dependency on technology and the risk of exposure to anti-social models in the form of violent computer games. Currently there is considerable evidence for the advantages of computer-aided learning and little research pointing to major problems.

Computers can be used to enhance learning in different ways. From a Vygotsky–Brunerian perspective, on-screen instructions from computers constitute scaffolding (Crook, 1994). When children use educational software the computer provides detailed help or prompts as required according to the child's position in the ZPD. Certain children in the class are inevitably more skilled in the use of computers and so take on the role of peer tutors. With pupils working on computers, the teacher is free to target individuals who require help and target appropriate scaffolding to each child.

Papert (1980) has also suggested that children acquire new thinking skills when they learn to program computers. Papert was one of a team that developed a child-friendly programming language called Logo. One of the features of Logo is a turtle graphic that can be directed to draw lines by typed commands. For example the command FORWARD 70, RIGHT 90 would direct the turtle graphic to draw a 70 mm line then turn 90°. Papert proposed that using the turtle to draw lines enhances children's mathematical abilities. Papert was more influenced by Piaget than by Vygotsky and Bruner, and he believed that using Logo helped children's thinking by developing their abilities of formal operational thought as opposed to concrete operational thought. In line with Piaget's thinking, Papert suggested that the teacher's role in working with computers should be confined to creating a suitable environment for children to work within.

Since Papert's claims most researchers have failed to find that children trained in the use of Logo show any significant advantage in their thinking abilities over other children. However, a recent study by Kramarski and Mevarech (1997) showed that instructing students in **metacognitive skills** and then giving them Logo tasks did result in improvements in metacognition. Metacognition refers to the child's awareness of their own mental strategies for carrying out tasks. In the Kramarski and Mevarech study, 68 12 to 14-year-old students from an Israeli junior high school were randomly assigned to one of four computer classes. All the students studied a computer-based course in statistics using Logo for one 45-minute lesson a week over 30 weeks. Two of the classes had training in metacognition and two did not. Metacognitive training consisted of lessons in which the teacher explored with the students all their possible methods of solving problems. At the end of the year the group instructed in metacognition performed better in their use of Logo and had enhanced their own metacognitive abilities – i.e. they had a better understanding of how they worked out and performed mental tasks.

A third way in which computers can enhance learning is in fostering social interaction. Mevarech *et al.* (1991) tested the idea that students working together sharing a computer will do better than students working alone. Researchers followed the progress of 12-year-olds working on computer-based arithmetic tasks for five months. Half the students had their own computer and the others shared a computer and worked in pairs. The latter group did significantly better when tested later on their arithmetic ability. This finding runs counter to common sense, which would predict that students who had their own computer would do better than those having to share. It also supports Vygotsky's view of learning as opposed to that of Piaget.

Contributions and limitations of the cognitive-developmental approach

- Psychologists like Piaget and Vygotsky have established firmly that children are not just little adults but that they have their own forms of thinking that are quite distinct from the ways our minds work as adults. This has given us an invaluable insight into child development.
- Cognitive-developmental theory has been applied successfully in the field of education. Modern teaching techniques ranging from individual discovery learning to computer-aided work in pairs has been influenced by the work of Piaget and Vygotsky.
- There are other situations in which it is helpful to have a good understanding of the way in which children think. These range from play-work, in which it is helpful to understand children's concepts of rules, to anaesthesiology (the study of pain and pain relief), where it is invaluable to have a grasp of children's understanding of the pain they are experiencing as a result of medical conditions and medical procedures.

Despite these invaluable contributions, a cognitive-developmental approach is not generally considered to be sufficient for a complete understanding of psychology, or even of child psychology. Some of its limitations include the following:

- From a psychodynamic perspective, the cognitive-developmental approach neglects the importance of children's emotional development. In a sense this is not a fair criticism of Piaget, who admired the work of Freud (see Chapter 3) and saw his own work as complementing rather than rivalling Freud's theories. However, it is fair to say that the cognitive-developmental approach does not really tackle emotional development, which is clearly of huge importance to children's psychological development.
- From a behavioural perspective (see Chapter 2), the cognitive-developmental approach overemphasises speculation about mental processes at the expense of more scientific research into the importance of conditioning in learning.

Summary

Cognitive-developmental psychology is an approach to understanding the development of logical thought, and the ways in which this impacts on our behaviour. The most influential theory in this area comes from Piaget, whose major contribution was in identifying the ways in which childhood logic differs from that of adults. Piaget also emphasised the process by which children explore and learn from their environment. Vygotsky broadly agreed with many of Piaget's ideas, but placed more emphasis on the importance of learning from others than learning by discovery. Both Piaget's and Vygotsky's ideas have been applied to teaching. The ideas of both Piaget and Vygotsky point towards an active role for pupils in their learning, but whereas followers of Piaget advocate solo discovery learning, educationalists influenced more by Vygotsky tend to prefer group work and more help by teachers and other learners. Computer-aided learning, a growth area in education, can be understood from the viewpoints of both Piaget and Vygotsky.

Think back to the vignettes in Chapter 1. Can a cognitive-developmental perspective add anything to our understanding of these cases?

Review exercise

Further reading

Lee, V. and Das Gupta, P. (1995) *Children's Cognitive and Language Development*, Milton Keynes: Open University. Covers a much broader area of cognitive development than is possible in this chapter, including the development of language and reading.

Smith, P.K., Cowie, H. and Blades, M. (1998) *Understanding Children's Development*, London: Blackwell. A very clear, although quite detailed and advanced, undergraduate-level text, featuring some great material on applying cognitive-developmental theory to education.

7

Social psychology

Key assumptions of the approach

Think back to someone you have spoken to in the last 24 hours. In what ways was your behaviour influenced by that person, and how might you have influenced them? Did you find them attractive or cool? If so, why? Did they belong to a group that you have positive or negative feelings about? If so, did you show your feelings? If not, why not, and how did you conceal your reactions to them? You begin to see the complexity of social psychology, but also its relevance to all of us. Every time we interact with someone else we are potentially involved in a huge number of social processes. When most people say they are interested in psychology it is really social psychology – the study of human interaction – that they mean.

The previous four chapters began with a typical study used to illustrate that particular approach. Trying to find a typical social-psychological study is a bit like trying to identify a typical person. They are simply too diverse. Social psychologists have used a tremendous variety of methods to investigate people's social behaviour. In this chapter we will be looking at research ranging from experiments in which participants are ordered to give people fatal electric shocks in order to see whether they will obey a person in authority (Milgram, 1963), to an analysis of the political implications of the language people use to talk about rape (Doherty and Anderson, 1998). Given that social approaches to psychology vary so widely, it is important to identify the key assumptions that tie social psychology together.

- *Social psychology is interested in all the ways in which people impact on one another.* For example, in the Milgram study mentioned above (and described in detail on pp. 123–124), orders from an authority figure affect the behaviour of participants.
- *The major influence on people's behaviour is the social situation they are in.* In the Milgram study, for example, participants found themselves in a social situation where they perceived that they had no choice but to obey a figure in authority.
- *Social approaches are not tied to a particular research method.* Whereas research in behavioural psychology consists mostly of experiments carried out in the psychology laboratory, and the majority of psychodynamic research involves case studies of patients in therapy, social psychologists use a wide variety of approaches to research.

Still (1998) has identified two traditional approaches to social psychology. **Psychological social psychology**, traditionally carried out by psychologists, has developed using largely experimental research. People are deliberately placed in particular social situations and their responses to those situations are systematically noted. This is a highly scientific psychology. **Sociological social psychology**, traditionally carried out by sociologists, differs in being less scientific and more concerned with political issues such as gender inequalities. In recent years a new approach called **social constructionism** has emerged as many psychologists have begun to adopt methods and ideas that were once considered to be part of sociology. Later in this chapter we will look at social constructionism in detail (see pp. 132–137). First, however, we shall look at the phenomenon of obedience, the study of which has been dominated by an experimental approach.

Obedience and agency

Adolf Eichmann was executed in 1962 for his part in organising the Holocaust, in which six million Jewish people, as well as gypsies, communists and trade unionists were transported to death camps and murdered in Nazi Germany and surrounding countries under Nazi control. Eichmann was a logistical genius whose part in the Holocaust was the planning of the efficient collection, transportation and extermination of those to be killed. At his trial in 1961, Eichmann expressed surprise at being hated by Jewish people, saying that he had merely obeyed orders, and surely obeying orders could only be a good thing. In his jail diary Eichmann wrote 'The orders were, for me, the highest thing in my life and I had to obey them without question' (extract quoted in *The Guardian*, 12 August, 1999, p. 13). Eichmann was declared sane by six psychiatrists, he had a normal family life and observers at his trial described him as very average. Given that there appears to be nothing particularly unusual about Eichmann, we must face the uncomfortable possibility that his behaviour was the product of the social situation in which he found himself, and that under the right circumstances we may all be capable of monstrous acts.

Following the Second World War – and in particular the Holocaust – psychologists set out to investigate the phenomenon of human obedience. Early attempts to explain the Holocaust had focused on the idea that there was something distinctive about German culture that had allowed the Holocaust to take place. Stanley Milgram set out to test the research question 'are Germans different?', but he quickly found that we are all surprisingly obedient to people in authority. In one of the most famous series of experiments in psychology, Milgram (1963–74) demonstrated that most participants would give a helpless victim fatal electric shocks when ordered to. The original study is described here in detail.

KEY STUDY: S. Milgram (1963) Behavioural study of obedience. *Journal of Abnormal and Social Psychology* 67, 371–378.

Aim: Following the Holocaust, Milgram set out to investigate how obedient people would be in a situation where following orders would mean breaking the moral code of the participant and harming another person.

Method: Milgram advertised for male volunteers to take part in an experiment on learning for a fee of $5. When they arrived at the university, participants were told they would be either a teacher or a learner. They were introduced to 'Mr Wallace', who was in fact an actor working for Milgram. By fudging an apparently random procedure, Milgram ensured that the participant was always the teacher and Mr Wallace always the learner. Mr Wallace was then strapped into a chair and given a memory task involving remembering pairs of words. Every time the learner made a mistake Milgram ordered the participant to give him an electric shock. Of course there were no real shocks, but there was no way for the participant to realise this. Following each mistake the size of the 'shock' increased. The shock levels on the machine were labelled from 0–450 volts and additionally had signs saying 'danger – severe shock' and, at 450 volts 'XXX'. Milgram ordered participants to continue giving increased shocks whilst the learner shouted and screamed in pain then appeared to collapse. When participants protested Milgram told them 'the experiment requires that you continue'.

Results: All participants gave Mr Wallace some electric shocks and 65 per cent went the distance, giving the full 450 volts to an apparently dead Mr Wallace. Most participants protested and some wept and begged in their distress, fully believing that they had killed Mr Wallace. However, most people did not feel that they could stop when ordered to continue by Milgram.

Discussion

This dramatic study demonstrates the power of authority over our behaviour. What is particularly interesting is that participants were very upset by what they had to do, but saw no alternative except to obey. Several other universities replicated the study and found similar results. Milgram has been criticised for the ethics of this study because he deceived participants, caused them great distress and did not allow them to leave the study when they asked to.* He was in fact briefly suspended from the American Psychological Association for his conduct of this study, but after an enquiry he was reinstated and his research approved. Another criticism is that Milgram underestimated the importance of individual differences in obedience. Some people are much more likely to resist orders than others, and this important fact was neglected by Milgram.

* Before conducting any psychological research, you must consult the guidelines for ethics in research published by the British Psychological Society or the Association for the Teaching of Psychology. Replications of the Milgram study by students are *not* considered acceptable.

One question asked following the Milgram studies was whether women would have the same tendency to obey when it meant harming someone – remember that Milgram's participants were male. Blass (1993) reviewed eight studies and noted that seven of them found identical rates of obedience for men and women.

Other studies, including those carried out in real-life settings, have confirmed that people have a remarkable tendency to obey those in authority. Bushman (1988) performed an experiment in a real-life setting where a female researcher, dressed either in a police-type uniform, as a business executive or as a beggar told people in the street to give change to a male researcher for a parking meter. Seventy-two per cent of people obeyed when she was dressed in uniform. As expected, fewer people obeyed in the other conditions. Interestingly, being dressed as a business executive or a beggar made very little difference – rates were 48 and 52 per cent respectively. Hence people appeared not to be simply responding to the social status of the person giving the order. When interviewed afterwards participants tended to report that they had obeyed the woman in uniform simply because she appeared to have authority.

Agency theory

Milgram (1974) proposed that we have evolved the tendency to obey those in authority as a way of maintaining a stable society. Clearly for humans to exist in a complex society we need social rules, and sticking to rules requires that at least some of the time we give up some of our free will. Milgram proposed that we have evolved two social states. In the autonomous state we are free to act as we wish, including how our conscience dictates. However, when our agentic state kicks in we surrender free will and conscience in the interests of serving the wider group. When we are in an agentic state we see ourselves as the agents of those in authority rather than being responsible for our actions.

We are socialised into developing an agentic state during childhood. In school for example, children learn to put aside their individual impulses in favour of maintaining order and so catering for the good of the class as a whole. Milgram proposed that, like children in class, we are all constantly subordinating our own needs and wishes to those of wider society. We can see this tendency in how people act in their jobs. In principle most people would say that they work for their own benefit and would not go out of their way for their employers. In reality, however, once people are in a job and they identify themselves as part of an organisation, they tend to put the needs of the organisation above their own.

An important aspect of the agentic state is the way we deal with moral strain. Moral strain results when we have to do something we believe to be morally wrong in order to function as an agent of authority, working for the good of society. Milgram suggested that we use psychological defence mechanisms (including those proposed by Freud – see Chapter 3) to get around the distress of having to do morally wrong things. Denial was particularly common in participants in the Milgram studies and in the Holocaust as perpetrators refused to confront what they were doing. It has been widely reported that guards at the Nazi concentration camps were supplied unlimited quantities of alcohol and that they stayed constantly drunk in order to help them deny the horror in which they were participating.

Evaluation of agency theory

If we accept that behaviour can be a product of evolution (we will examine this is detail in Chapter 8), then it is quite possible that we have evolved the tendency to obey those in authority in order to help create stable societies. Agency theory does explain a wide range of social behaviours, ranging from how we act at work to the way in which peaceful people can go to war, and of course how 'normal' people become involved in ethnic cleansing. Results of studies like that of Bushman (1988) support agency theory because they show that a major factor in determining whether people will obey orders is whether they identify the person giving the order as an authority figure.

Some aspects of agency theory are rather vague and difficult to test however. For example, Milgram's idea of an agentic state is an interesting idea but difficult to investigate in practice. Agency theory, like Milgram's research, neglects the importance of individual differences in obedience. Some people simply will not obey orders if they don't want to, and this is hard to account for by the evolution of an agentic state.

Prejudice and social identity

Like obedience, prejudice is central to our social behaviour. We all have a strong tendency to adopt attitudes to things, people and groups we encounter. Prejudices can be defined as extreme attitudes. Like all attitudes, prejudices consist of three elements: cognitive, emotional and behavioural. The cognitive component of an attitude consists of beliefs about the target group. The emotional element consists of feelings towards the target group and the behavioural element involves action towards the target group. For example, if we hold a prejudice against football fans we might believe they are violent, feel afraid of them and avoid going out near football grounds after a match.

1 For the above example of prejudice against football fans, identify the cognitive, emotional and behavioural components.
2 What groups can you identify that are particular targets of prejudice?

Progress exercise

Prejudices lead us to maximise the similarities between all members of a group and minimise the differences between individuals. Because of this we tend to make swift and often unjust judgements about people based on their membership of a group. This will lead to some sort of **discrimination**. Literally, discrimination just means treating people differently. In practice discrimination can be as apparently mild as avoiding football fans after a match or it can be extreme, resulting in violence, murder and, ultimately, **genocide**. In the previous section we looked at the part obedience had to play in the Holocaust. Clearly prejudice also played a major role in the Holocaust and in other instances of genocide. Whilst the Holocaust was unique in the *scale* of its genocide, there have been a great many instances of 'ethnic cleansing' before and since. At the time of writing the most recent highly publicised example of ethnic cleansing has taken place in Kosovo, where the Serbian population massacred and drove ethnic Albanians from the country. Incidentally, if you think that just avoiding people does no harm, think again! A study by Hunter and Ross (1991) revealed that many doctors, nurses and social workers spent less time with people with AIDS than they did with other patients. As well as increasing their feelings of alienation, this avoidance potentially endangered the patients as they received less care.

How prejudiced are we?

There have been many studies conducted to establish just how prejudiced people are, and towards whom they display prejudice. Racism is an example of a widespread prejudice. A Gallup poll of 959 white British people in 1993 (reported by Skellington, 1995) revealed that 25 per cent of people would object to living next door to a non-white person, and that 10 per cent wanted anti-racism laws to be abolished. On the other hand 40 per cent of people surveyed wanted the anti-racism laws strengthened. This shows that there is a wide spectrum of attitudes to race and racism. Whilst overtly racist attitudes were only present in a minority of white Britons, it was a very significant minority.

Worldwide, the group experiencing the most prejudice and discrimination is women (Baron and Byrne, 1994). Glick and Fiske (1996) surveyed 2,000 men and women using a questionnaire called the 'Ambivalent Sexism Inventory'. They identified two distinct types of prejudice against women. Hostile prejudice is typical of other prejudices, being characterised by strongly negative feelings of anger, dislike and contempt. Benevolent prejudice, on the other hand, involves a patronising benevolence towards women, liking them but expecting them to stay in their (submissive) place. A series of studies by Hatcher (1997) found that, although young people tended to state in principle that they believed in equality, when more specific questions were asked some sexist attitudes emerged. One of the three studies carried out by Hatcher is reported here.

KEY STUDY: D. Hatcher (1997) Male and female worlds: students' views of domestic tasks. *Psychology Teaching*, 5, 46–98.

Aim: Hatcher aimed to establish whether there was a difference in the attitudes of male and female students in further education towards the division of child-rearing tasks in couples. This was investigated by an attitude survey using a questionnaire.

Method: 112 students between the ages of 16 and 18 were selected by quota sampling (see Searle, 1999, for a discussion of sampling methods) from a rural British college of further education over a period of eight years. A questionnaire was administered one to one by a fellow student. The questionnaire consisted of 21 closed questions requiring yes/no or male/female responses and 12 open questions requiring longer answers. All the questions pertained to the division of work by gender in child-rearing. The first question was very general 'In bringing up children do you think both parents should be equally involved.' In a later item, participants were asked what child-rearing activities were particularly male or female.

Results: In response to the general question regarding whether both parents should be involved in child-rearing there was strong agreement between males and females: 97 per cent of females and 88 per cent of males expressed an intention to share all child-rearing tasks with their partner. However, when the questions got more specific gender differences emerged: 20 per cent of females and 29 per cent of males believed that men and women have different roles to play. Amongst female participants, women were seen as having roles of motherhood, keeping the family together, having children and being caring; men were typically identified as being the 'breadwinner' and focusing on work. Amongst the men who supported differing gender roles the emphasis seemed to be more on power relationships, and a frequent response was that men should be leaders and women subservient. Similarly, males were more likely to identify a male role in disciplining children and providing pocket money than females.

Discussion

This is an interesting study in that it shows up the fact that, although the young people professed to have non-sexist attitudes, some traditional male attitudes emerged under questioning. Hatcher concluded that it is too early to hail the appearance of the 'new man'. These male attitudes can be classified as benevolent prejudice, and this study supports Glick and Fiske (1996) in their belief that most prejudice against women is of this type, and that this makes sexism different from other prejudices. However, because the sample was relatively small for a study of this type, and because the differences between male and female responses were not great, further research is needed before we can reach any firm conclusions about the sexist attitudes of young people.

Although racism and sexism have been the most extensively studied forms of prejudice, there are many others. Skinner *et al.* (1995) surveyed Americans about their attitudes towards ex-psychiatric patients, ex-convicts and ex-drug-addicts. Questions centred on people's beliefs about the relationships, family, employment and social and psychological functioning of the three groups. It was found that the most serious prejudice was shown towards the ex-drug-addicts, followed by the ex-psychiatric patients. Ex-prisoners fared best. Having established that prejudice exists, the next question faced by psychologists is 'why?' One popular explanation comes from Tajfel and Turner's social identity theory.

Social identity theory

Tajfel and Turner (1979) have proposed that much of our social behaviour can be explained by our tendency to identify ourselves as part of a group, and to evaluate others as either within or outside that group. This means that we make a sharp judgement of people as either one of 'us' or one of 'them'. Although the nature of the groups we see ourselves as belonging to will vary widely according to our individual experience and the culture we live in, the tendency to think of ourselves as part of one or more groups is universal. Presumably, as social animals we have evolved the mechanisms of identifying with a group to aid cooperation and so help us form societies.

Tajfel and Turner proposed that there are three cognitive processes involved in evaluating others as 'us' or 'them'. These take place in a particular order. They are shown in Figure 7.1.

In the first stage, social categorisation, we identify ourselves and

Figure 7.1 **The three-stage process in social identity theory**

other people as members of social categories. Categories we all tend to subscribe to include gender, race and class. Others are more relevant to some people than others – for example, football-supporting and cat-loving. Although the categories we consider most important vary according to the individual, we do not make up categories as individuals. Instead we take categories that we have learned to be important. We can of course categorise ourselves as part of several groups. You can thus be a psychologist, a martial artist and a cat-lover without any conflict. However, as a cat-lover you may tend to see other cat-lovers as an in-group and dog-lovers as an out-group.

In the second stage, **social identification**, we adopt the identity of the group we have categorised ourselves as belonging to. If for example you have categorised yourself as a student, the chances are you will adopt the identity of a student and begin to act in the ways you believe students act. There will be an emotional significance to your identification with a group, and your self-esteem will become bound up with group membership.

The final stage is **social comparison**. Once we have categorised ourselves as part of a group and identified with that group we then tend to compare that group with other groups. If our self-esteem is to be maintained our group needs to compare favourably with other groups. This is critical to understanding prejudice, because once two groups identify themselves as rivals they are forced to compete in order for the members to maintain their self-esteem. Competition and hostility between groups is thus not only a matter of competing for resources like jobs but also the result of competing identities. This does not mean of course that there is nothing we can do to reduce prejudice. We shall return to the issue of reducing prejudice later in this chapter (see pp. 137–140).

Evaluation of social identity theory

Social identity theory explains a whole host of social phenomena, ranging from racism to mate selection, from class conflict to the camaraderie of following a football club or band. Social identity theory has also been applied to understanding psychology itself. Jarvis (2000) has suggested that as psychologists and psychology students we tend to favour psychological approaches that fall within mainstream psychology because we identify their authors as an in-group. Thus the theories of behavioural and cognitive psychologists tend to be popular because they are easily identified as within psychology. Psychodynamic theorists, who are generally not psychologists but members of out-groups such as psychiatrists and psychoanalysts, often receive a much harder time in psychology, at least partly because of their out-group status.

Despite its usefulness, social identity theory is not without its critics. Like Milgram's agency theory, social identity theory tends to underestimate the importance of individual differences. Some people have a much greater tendency than others to favour in-groups over out-groups, depending on their personality. Cross-cultural research has also shown that not all cultures display the same tendency to favour in-groups as we do in Europe and America (Wetherall, 1997).

Social constructionism

This is a radical approach to psychology which, although it meets the key assumptions for social psychology discussed at the start of this chapter, differs in several important ways from the mainstream social psychology we have looked at so far. Social constructionism questions the scientific and non-political nature of psychology, traditional research methods and the very nature of reality itself. This is complex stuff, so let us look at each of these issues in turn.

A deliberately political and unscientific psychology?

Social constructionists disagree with the traditional view of psychologists that our job is to make objective and unbiased observations about people. In fact social constructionists do not believe that it is possible to be objective or make unbiased observations because we can only see the world as it is represented in our culture and language. This effectively means that the aims of science are unrealistic. Social constructionists do not necessarily reject the idea of scientific research and knowledge entirely, but they do emphasise strongly that so-called science is as rooted in cultural beliefs and practices as any other human endeavour and that the scientific assumption of objectivity is naive.

Social constructionism is often intentionally political. Whereas most psychologists would see their work as uncovering scientific knowledge, social constructionists see their role as more to uncover and challenge social inequality and injustice. Social constructionist explanations of psychological phenomena look at social and historical reasons why ideas might have emerged, with particular regard to power relationships between groups. For example, traditional assumptions about gender include the idea of women as submissive, gentle and caring. A social constructionist would probably say that femininity has been constructed in this way, so that women will serve the needs of men without challenging the male-dominated society. Similarly, by defining a group such as the middle classes or white Americans as 'more intelligent' than other groups, by virtue of the fact that they tend to score more highly on IQ tests (which are of course biased towards the knowledge and skills of white middle-class people), white middle-class Americans strengthen their own power relative to other groups in society.

The importance of culture and language

The way we understand the world is determined by our culture. This is why we cannot make objective and unbiased observations of people. Rather than there being a set of facts to discover about the world, social constructionists see the world we perceive as being *socially constructed*. Psychological concepts like childhood, intelligence and mental illness are thus not fixed in reality, but are whatever we as a culture agree them to be. Language is extremely important in social constructionism, because the type of language we use to describe something influences our perception of it. A simple example is the way we use the word 'intelligence'. Whilst we certainly have cognitive abilities, and whilst some people are better at some cognitive tasks than others, a social constructionist would say that the idea of intelligence as a *thing* which can be measured, and which one person can have more of than another, is a social construct.

Discourse and discourse analysis

We have already said that language is of huge importance in how we construct our view of the world. Discourse literally means whatever people say or write. There can be several alternative discourses around concerning a single subject, each of which gives that subject a different meaning. Burr (1995) says that each discourse is 'a set of meanings, metaphors, representations, images, stories, statements and so on that in some way together produce a particular version of events' (p. 48). Burr gives the example of fox-hunting. Those who favour fox-hunting tend to speak of it as pest-control, using a traditional, natural method. Alternative discourses around fox-hunting from those against it might involve speaking of it as fundamentally immoral or a decadent pastime of the idle rich. These different *discourses* construct entirely different meanings to fox-hunting.

The major research method of social constructionism is **discourse analysis**. By looking at discourse in the form of conversation, writing and music, psychologists can 'unpack' many of the assumptions we have about the world. A classic example of this comes from Doherty and Anderson (1998), in their analysis of conversations about rape. We can look at this in detail.

KEY STUDY: K. Doherty and I. Anderson (1998) Perpetuating rape-supportive culture: talking about rape. *The Psychologist* 11 (12), 583–587.

Aim: The researchers analysed three conversations in order to unpack the ways in which blame was attributed to victims of rape. This attributing of blame to victims is critical for two reasons. First, victims of rape tend to be blamed and this can cause them additional and avoidable heartache (this is called secondary victimisation). Second, attaching even part of the blame to the victims of rape perpetuates a culture in which the crime of rape is to some extent condoned.

Conversation: Pairs of men and women were given a description of a hypothetical rape. The conversations following this were recorded and analysed. A section of one conversation is shown below:

1 Vernon: *Well yeah so here we're saying that she should have probably been aware of this and not been so foolish as to take a shortcut, but even so . . .*
2 Sally: *Maybe . . . she . . . yeah it does seem that way doesn't it, they should be able to I think.*

3 Vernon: *Yeah but even so . . . People should be able to walk about in freedom but . . .*

4 Sally: *But the trouble is you can't nowadays can you . . . I mean it's too dangerous.*

5 Vernon: *Well . . .*

6 Sally: *I mean people are forever telling you on television you know whatever you don't.*

7 Vernon: *Yeah; I think people are becoming more and more aware of it.*

Discourse analysis: The speakers jointly construct a version of the world (*nowadays*, line 4) in which it is normal for people to be attacked. It is suggested (line 7) that people are increasingly realising how dangerous the world is, therefore there is no excuse for the victim not to have been aware of her danger. It is further suggested that it is quite possible to predict being attacked (line 1, *taking a shortcut*), and that it is easy to avoid being attacked by simply walking home a different way. This suggests in turn that the victim was *foolish* (line 1). The victim is thus constructed by the speakers' use of language as someone who knew the danger and how to avoid it, but who stupidly *put herself* in danger. Thus blame for the rape is firmly laid at the door of the victim.

Discussion

This extract shows clearly that these two people have talked themselves round to a position where they are attributing at least part of the blame for the rape to the victim. She is spoken of not as a victim of violence but as someone who should have known better, and who was foolish and negligent in her own behaviour. The other two conversations analysed by the researchers revealed similar attitudes. The analysis of these conversations reveals a key to understanding and tackling secondary victimisation of rape victims, and ultimately making society less tolerant of rape.

Discourse and reality

If social constructionists aim to uncover the different versions of reality we can identify in discourse we are left with an awkward question. Is there really such a thing as reality? There are different beliefs about this within social constructionism. The most extreme constructionists would deny that there is any reality at all, and that we construct the world entirely through discourse. As Burr (1998) says, however, this can be a dangerous path, for two reasons. First, if we accept that there are different and equally valid versions of reality how do we choose between them? Second, if we accept that any version of reality can be equally valid, do we say that any discourse is acceptable, however antisocial? There are, for example, historians who claim that the Holocaust never happened, although the reality is unquestionably that it did. Furthermore, if there is no reality, any injustice becomes okay, as long as we can put a positive 'spin' on it. You should be aware however that the idea that there is *no* reality is extreme, even within social constructionism, and that most constructionists believe that there *is* reality but that our perceptions of it are distorted by language.

Evaluation of social constructionism

Because social constructionism is such a growth area at the time of writing, it is impossible to say whether it will turn out to be a brief trend or the shape of psychology to come. On the one hand, research into how language shapes our perceptions of reality has enriched our understanding of what makes people 'tick' and has had valuable practical applications, such as understanding the secondary victimisation of rape victims. Later in this chapter we can have a brief look at the role discourse analysis has played in tackling racism. Social constructionism has also made psychologists take a step back from their traditional assumptions about reality, science and knowledge, and to look more broadly at the social and political implications of what they do.

As you might expect, those who see psychology as a pure science tend to be reluctant to accept that the social constructionist perspective has much virtue. To the scientist, arguments about the nature of reality are simply an irrelevant self-indulgence. To reject all the understandings and practical applications of traditional psychology just on the basis of philosophical arguments is surely to throw out the baby with the bathwater on a grand scale. In defence of traditional social psychology, McGhee (1998) has pointed out that traditional psychologists are aware of their weaknesses as identified by social constructionists, but that being realistic more can generally be accomplished by a scientific approach.

Key application: tackling racism

There are a number of psychological approaches to tackling racism. For reasons of space we cannot look at all these approaches, but, based on some of the ideas we have already looked at in this chapter, we can examine two approaches. Gaertner's common in-group identity model is based on social identity theory. Based on social constructionism we can also look at how we might identify and replace racist discourse so that people will begin to construct their perceptions of 'race' differently.

Common in-group identity model

Gaertner *et al.* (1989) proposed an approach to reducing racism based on social identity theory. If one cause of prejudice is our instinctive tendency to classify people as either part of our group or outside it, then we should in principle be able to reduce racism if we make people start to see people from different cultural groups as part of a single group. According to Gaertner, weakening us-and-them boundaries should begin a process where more positive attitudes lead to an increase in contact between groups. From there prejudice should naturally reduce. This begs the question 'How do we get people to redraw their boundaries so that different cultural groups are perceived as one group?' According to Gaertner one way is to establish cooperative interaction between groups. This means getting groups to work together towards achieving the same goal. In one experiment, Gaertner *et al.* (1990) demonstrated that cooperative interaction leads people to redraw in-group out-group boundaries. The researchers established two groups of three people each. In one condition the two groups were brought into contact so that they could work together. In another condition, the two groups were brought into contact but did not work together. When the groups were surveyed about their perceptions of who was in the group, the groups who had worked together identified themselves as one group of six, whereas the groups who had not worked together identified themselves as two groups of three.

Of course laboratory experiments like the one above lack *ecological validity* – i.e. they are not representative of real-world situations. There is a huge difference between groups put together for an experiment and naturally occurring cultural groups who have identified themselves as distinct groups for their whole lives and who may have experienced conflict with other groups. However, a later study does show that in real-life settings people's experience of cooperative interaction is related to their perception of themselves as one large group rather than several small groups. Gaertner *et al.* (1993) gave 1,300 pupils at a multicultural American high school a survey that measured cooperative interaction and attitudes to their own and other cultural groups. It was found that the pupils that had engaged in most cooperative interaction were most likely to identify the pupils at the school as a single body rather than several smaller cultural groups.

The idea of breaking down barriers between cultural groups by giving them shared tasks is appealing, and in situations where it is practical is probably quite effective. In situations such as schools, where different cultural groups mix and are engaged in the same type of tasks, the common in-group identity model is a good approach to improving intergroup relations. The limitation of this model is, however, fairly obvious. Once two groups have actually fallen out, and are engaged in hostilities towards each other, it would be extremely difficult to persuade them to come together in common aims. This approach is perhaps most effective as a preventive way of tackling racism, for example in school.

Racist discourse

From a social constructionist perspective, racism is perpetuated by our use of language. You may have noticed that in this section I have avoided using terms like 'race' and 'ethnic'. This is not an accident, not because these terms are unfashionable but because I fear that when we define differences between cultural groups as 'racial' we are constructing the groups as in some way innately and absolutely different from one another. The term 'race' has no scientific meaning, but strong connotations. A 'racial difference' in some social-psychological variable (for example child-rearing) sounds as if it is as much a part of the 'race' concerned as skin colour. By contrast, when we speak of 'cultural' differences we appear to be speaking of much smaller, less immutable differences. One simple way in which we can begin to change discourse to make it less likely to perpetuate racism is to avoid speaking of racial differences when what we are really concerned with is differences in culture.

Another way in which discourse can be reconstructed so as to reduce racism is to speak of groups in terms of adjectives rather than nouns. If we describe someone as 'a Black' (noun) we are constructing a *thing* which appears to be in some way a Black as opposed to a normal person. By contrast, to say 'a Black person' (adjective) describes a *person* (with all the individuality and rights that go with being a person), who happens to be black. You can see that using words like 'black' as adjectives rather than nouns helps to present people in a positive light, and many people including newsreaders, politicians and psychologists have shifted towards this.

Racism can be embedded in discourse in other ways. Condor (1988) described how, in the Conservative Party manifesto for the 1987 General Election, 'race' is linked with crime. Under a general heading of 'Freedom, law and responsibility' the subheading 'race' appeared with other subheadings of 'the fight against crime' and 'tackling drug abuse'. This clearly identifies Black people as a problem on a par with crime and drugs, and perhaps even as *associated* with crime and drugs. As Wetherall (1997) says, this kind of link can become so well established that people will make the leap between 'Black' and 'mugger' automatically.

The discourse of psychology is not immune from racism. Owusu-Bempah and Howitt (1994) have analysed the language used in leading American psychology texts and found numerous examples of language that in subtle ways risk perpetuating racism. Taking *Introduction to Psychology*, by Atkinson *et al.* (1993) as an example, Owusu-Bempah and Howitt identified language that portrayed people other than Westerners as strange, undifferentiated (i.e. all the same) and primitive. The word 'tribe' is frequently used when describing a group of non-Western people. However, as the researchers point out, *Chambers Twentieth Century Dictionary* defines a tribe as 'a race, a breed, a class of people; groups of animals usually ranking between a genus and an order'. Elsewhere in the book, Atkinson *et al.* use the word 'tribe' to describe a group of chimpanzees. This means that – quite unintentionally but powerfully – the authors are linking Black people with chimpanzees rather than to other humans. *Introduction to Psychology* also illustrates cultural differences in social behaviours using examples that portray Africans as barbaric. For example, it is claimed that among the Ashanti, sex with a girl who has not undergone puberty rites is punished by death for both participants. As well as being a bad example of a cultural difference because it needlessly portrays African people as barbaric, it is, according to Owusu-Bempah and Howitt, completely untrue!

There is of course a gap between identifying racist discourse and doing away with racism. However, if we can identify and remove some of the racism in discourse we may go some way towards helping construct their views of the world in a less racist way. Those who have not studied discourse analysis often scoff at the use of 'politically correct' language. However, if we accept that (at least to some extent) people construct their world through language, it is well worth trying to eliminate language that encourages racist attitudes. Although a long-term approach, exposing and eliminating racist discourse will probably help in the reduction of racism.

Progress exercise

Look at some of the discourses that have helped shape your view of the world. You might want to look at the news (written or broadcast) or, if you are a student, the textbooks you use. What racist discourse can you identify?

Contemporary issue: lesbian and gay psychology

Traditionally psychology has tended to either ignore lesbian and gay people or treat them as abnormal. Indeed, until 1974 the Diagnostic and Statistical Manual of Mental Disorder (a system for describing and diagnosing mental disorders) included homosexuality as a mental disorder! Attitudes have changed to the extent that most people today would consider that to be ridiculous, but, even so, much research has continued to centre around explaining *why* some people are homosexual. This still identifies homosexuality as a thing that needs to be justified. Incidentally the term 'homosexuality' is a problematic one. It is associated with negative stereotypes and the idea of gay and lesbian people as somehow deviant. The term *lesbian and gay psychology* has become the internationally accepted term for the psychological study of gay and lesbian issues. The term *gay psychologist* describes the psychologist's area of study and not his/her sexual orientation.

In 1999 the British Psychological Society set up a lesbian and gay section, with the purposes of improving psychology's understanding of people and to use psychology to improve the lives of lesbians and gay men and their friends and families. Kitzinger *et al.* (1998) set out the following aims of the section. Psychologists can research gay and lesbian identities, and, through therapy, help individuals attain healthy identities, for example overcoming their own homophobia. They can also help people better understand gay and lesbian relationships and identify particular issues in gay and lesbian lifespan development. These areas of research are important in understanding human diversity and ceasing to assume that what we know from research on heterosexual identity, relationships and lifespan development is applicable to everyone.

On a practical level, psychologists can also contribute to explaining and tackling homophobia. Homophobia, the tendency to react negatively to lesbians and gay men, is believed to be a major source of stress, anxiety and depression in lesbians and gay men. In Chapter 3 we looked at a study by Adams *et al.* (1996) that showed that homophobic men were more aroused by gay pornography than non-homophobic men. This type of approach is unpopular with gay psychologists because, ultimately, it explains homophobia as something wrong with the individual. Most gay psychologists prefer to emphasise the social factors that give rise to homophobia.

Gay and lesbian psychology has come a long way from the days when homosexuality was labelled a mental disorder. It now has a firm research agenda dedicated to understanding human diversity and bettering the lives of lesbians and gay men and those associated with them. One of the reasons why this shift has been possible is that gay and lesbian psychology is now firmly located within social psychology. When psychologists emphasise social rather than individual factors it becomes possible to study an area without stigmatising the individuals concerned. This is perhaps one of the greatest contributions of the social approach to psychology.

Contributions and limitations of social approaches

Social psychology gives us a radically different perspective on human nature as opposed to other perspectives. The following are particularly important contributions:

- Social psychology has shown the impact that other people have on us, whether they be individuals, groups or society as a whole. Through social psychology we understand that the social situation is a powerful influence on our behaviour.
- Social psychology has developed a range of useful research techniques, including social experiments, conducting surveys and discourse analysis. It has also given rise to many practical applications, including ways to tackle racism and the secondary victimisation of rape victims.
- By shifting the emphasis of theory and research away from the individual and towards social processes, social psychology has allowed us to look at psychological phenomena in ways which do not pathologise the individual. A good example of this is the development of lesbian and gay psychology which, by adopting a social approach, has moved psychology away from explaining or justifying homosexuality and towards examining the psychological issues of importance to lesbians and gay men.
- Social psychology can tell us much about the rest of psychology. Social constructionism makes us look at the idea of psychology as science in a new way, and social identity theory tells us much about the attitudes of psychologists to rival professions and those using different theoretical approaches.

There is one principal limitation to adopting a purely social approach to psychology:

- Social psychologists' emphasis on social factors in affecting behaviour is sometimes at the expense of individual factors. All the major theories we have looked at in this chapter, including agency theory, social identity theory and social constructionism, tend to neglect the individual. Not all people respond in the same way to social influences and social situations, and these individual differences require explanations from other perspectives.

Summary

Social psychology is a wide field, taking as its central assumption the idea that the major influences on behaviour are social – i.e. arising from other people. We have looked at two social-psychological phenomena – obedience and prejudice – and one traditional explanation for each. The study of obedience and prejudice are traditional areas of social psychology. Of particular interest in psychology at the turn of the century is the new and radical approach of social constructionism. This is a deliberately non-scientific and political psychology that explains psychological phenomena as having been constructed for political reasons. The major research method of social constructionism is discourse analysis, which picks apart our use of language to show how we construct a shared perception of the world. A key application of social psychology is tackling racism. Two approaches, the common in-group identity model and the elimination of racist discourse, promise a long-term reduction in racism. A contemporary issue for social psychology is the development of lesbian and gay psychology. Adopting a social rather than an individual approach to lesbian and gay issues has meant that psychology has shifted from trying to explain or justify homosexuality to exploring the issues relevant to gay and lesbian people.

Look back at the three vignettes in Chapter 1. Now that you know a little more about social approaches to psychology, reflect on how well social theory explains each of these scenarios. You may find it helpful to note down what aspects of each situation a social approach can explain fully, and where it runs into difficulties.

Review exercise

Further reading

Burr, V. (1995) *An Introduction to Social Constructionism*, London: Routledge. A brilliantly readable though detailed and comprehensive guide to the rapid growth area of social constructionism.

Hayes, N. (1998) *Foundations of Psychology* (2nd edn), Walton-on-Thames: Nelson. My personal favourite of the big general textbooks for social psychology. Good, clear accounts of many of the issues covered here, and of course many other aspects of social psychology.

Wetherall, M. (ed.) (1997) *Identities, Groups and Social Issues*, London: Sage. An excellent account of European social psychology, including particularly good chapters on discourse and the psychology of racism

8

Biological psychology 1: genetic influences on behaviour

Key assumptions of the approach

Have you ever wondered why a particular characteristic like high IQ or perhaps a bad temper seems to run in your family? Thinking about people more generally, have you ever considered why people prefer to go to the toilet alone, or why a young man going out with an older woman raises eyebrows whereas no one looks twice at an older man partnered with a young woman? Although there are many possible explanations for these patterns, there has recently been an upsurge of interest in biological explanations for these and many other psychological phenomena. Over the next two chapters we shall look at three major concepts from biology that have proved useful in explaining human psychology – genetics, evolution and neurophysiology.

Genetics is the study of inheritance, and has been applied to psychology in looking at the extent to which psychological characteristics are affected by inheritance from parents. **Evolution** refers to ways in which a species changes in its genetic make-up over many generations. This idea can be applied to psychology by suggesting that psychological phenomena ranging from language to monogamy (remaining with a single mate) are the products of evolution.

Before we go on to look in more detail at the study of inheritance and evolution in psychology, let us just tie this chapter together by looking at what broad assumptions underlie the genetically based approaches to psychology:

- *Like behavioural and cognitive psychology, behavioural genetics and evolutionary psychology are seen as pure-science approaches.* They draw on concepts from the hard sciences and research tends to be highly scientific in nature.
- *Genes affect physical characteristics, and the interaction of these characteristics with the environment can influence psychological characteristics.* There may thus be genes that indirectly affect all human behaviour, and genes which influence individual psychological differences between people.
- *Whereas all the approaches we have looked at so far emphasise the role of the environment in determining the differences between people, behavioural genetics emphasises the role of genetic as well as environmental influences.* If for example your family tend to have high IQ or bad tempers, this would be explained by a combination of shared genes and shared environment.
- *Evolutionary psychology also emphasises the importance of genetic influences, but on human similarity rather than difference.* Thus the reason people generally like to go to the toilet alone could be explained from an evolutionary perspective as having evolved in order to prevent picking up germs from other people's excreta.

Let us now go on to look at behavioural genetics in detail, focusing on the issue of the extent to which intelligence is genetically determined. We can then look at evolutionary psychology, focusing on the possible evolutionary basis of our abilities in infancy and of adult social behaviour. We can then look at the contemporary issue of whether behavioural genetics poses a threat to the other approaches to psychology.

Behavioural genetics: the genetics of individual differences

Behavioural genetics is the study of the origins of the psychological differences between people. There are essentially two factors that can affect individual differences: genes and environment. These are sometimes called 'nature' and 'nurture' because your genetic make-up is determined by biology (hence nature), whereas your environment is controlled principally by other people (hence nurture). The *nature–nurture debate* is the general debate in psychology about the relative importance of genes and environment. Behavioural geneticists research the importance of both nature and nurture. Don't fall into the common trap of assuming that behavioural geneticists are out to prove we are entirely controlled by our genes.

We all share about 99.9 per cent of our genes – that is what makes us human. When we talk about genetic differences between individuals we are talking of just 0.1 per cent of our genes. None the less, this is sufficient to account for substantial differences between people. Characteristics that are largely under the control of genes are said to be high in **heritability**. Height is an example of a highly heritable characteristic. Manners on the other hand are low in heritability, because, as common sense tells us, the main influence on how polite we are is our upbringing. Unfortunately, psychology is rarely this simple, and the heritability of more complex psychological variables like intelligence and mental disorder remains an ongoing area of study and controversy.

The origins of intelligence

In Chapter 7 we looked at the idea that, from the perspective of social constructionism, the concept of intelligence as a thing of which one person can have more of than someone else is a misleading social construct. Suspend that idea for the time being, and think instead about individual differences in *cognitive abilities*. Psychologists measure individual cognitive abilities, for example by means of IQ (intelligence quotient) tests. It seems likely that there are both genetic and environmental influences on our individual levels of cognitive ability. Traditionally, behavioural geneticists have investigated the role of genes and environment in the development of individual cognitive ability by three methods: twin studies, family studies and adoption studies. For reasons of space we shall just look at twin studies here.

Twin studies

Twin studies take advantage of the fact that we know that mono-zygotic (MZ or identical) twins are genetically identical. Logic tells us therefore that any differences in their cognitive abilities must be environmental in origin. Separated identical twins provide us with a naturally occurring experimental condition of shared genes and different environment. If separated identical twins have similar IQs in spite of different environments this is powerful evidence for a role for genes in the development of cognitive ability.

We can also compare the similarity of IQ in identical twins and dizygotic (DZ or fraternal) twins, who share half of the 99.9 per cent of the genes that distinguish individual humans. If identical twins are more similar than fraternal twins in IQ, this provides further support for the importance of genetic factors in determining individual cognitive ability.

Studies exist that appear to support both these predictions – that separated identical twins have similar IQs and that identical twins are more similar than fraternal twins. Early studies suggested a very major role for genes (see Table 8.1). The results shown in Table 8.1, if taken at face value, suggest that genetic variation accounts for over 70 per cent of the variance in IQ. However, there are flaws with this type of study (based on Howe, 1997):

- In many cases 'separated' identical twins actually had extremely similar environments. Some had in fact been raised in the same family – even the same house – and went to the same school, seeing each other every day.
- In some cases twins had not been separated until several years after birth; thus they shared their early environment.
- In some studies such as Newman *et al.* (1937), *experimenter bias* accounted for some of the differences between groups of twins – those testing the twins for IQ knew which were identical and fraternal and which had been separated and which reared together.
- In many cases separated twins were tested some time after they had been reunited for some time. There is some evidence to suggest that reunited twins become more similar after being reunited.

Table 8.1 Results of early twin studies			
Study correlations	MZs reared together	MZs reared apart	DZs
Newman *et al.* (1937)	0.91	0.67	0.64
Shields (1962)	0.76	0.77	0.51

Of course we must remember that twin studies reliably show that identical twins reared apart are less similar in IQ than those reared together. This clearly indicates that environment also accounts for some of the variance in IQ. Plomin (1988) reviewed a large number of recent twin studies and concluded that they generally pointed to roughly equal importance of nature and nurture.

The nature–nurture debate around intelligence has evolved throughout the twentieth century. In the early 1900s when intelligence tests were first developed the argument was a simple one – is intelligence determined by genetics or environment? By the latter half of the century it was clear that both nature and nurture played a role, and the argument shifted to determining the relative importance of genetics and environment. In the 1990s, having accepted that nature and nurture are both important determinants of intelligence, researchers have begun a new endeavour to see *how* genetics and environment *interact* to produce the cognitive abilities of each individual.

Gene–environment interaction

Scarr (1992) has proposed a theory that sees most of the variance in intelligence and other individual differences as coming ultimately from genetics, although there is not a simple genetic basis to intelligence *per se*. This is possible because Scarr believes we tend to *create* our own environment, and the type of environment we create will be a *product* of our innate characteristics. This is a radical departure from a common-sense view that would say that as young children we are at the mercy of the environment provided by others. Scarr explains this in three ways:

- *Gene–environment correlation*: Scarr proposed that the only reason that we find correlations between environmental variables and later intelligence is because parents provide both the environment and the genes – so the quality of environment and genes inevitably correlate. However, it is the genes and not the environment that leads to the intelligence.

- *Evocation of responses*: Scarr proposed that different children *evoke* different treatment from adults, thus creating their own social and intellectual environment. From a very early age, sociable infants evoke more social interactions from caregivers, thus receiving more stimulation. This pattern continues in school where bright children may attract more attention from teachers.
- *Choice of environment*: Once past infancy, children have a degree of choice in what environment they seek out. As adults we select our environment in the form of education, occupation and leisure according to our preferences for certain levels and types of stimulation.

Scarr points out that very poor environments which fall outside the **average expectable environment** can still have negative effects on children because the opportunity to influence their environment is denied by neglect or abuse. However, provided parenting falls into the bounds of the average expectable environment, there is no reason why parenting styles should affect cognitive or social development.

Evaluation of Scarr's theory

Scarr's approach offers a credible explanation of how the behaviour of individuals, from a very early age, affects their environment. She has further offered a clever explanation for correlations between early environment and later IQ, other than the obvious conclusion that environment directly affects IQ. The idea that children evoke their environment rather than just passively receive treatment by others has become highly influential in child psychology.

Scarr's theory has received much criticism however, and alternative approaches to gene–environment interaction have been proposed. From a perspective of social responsibility, Scarr's assertion that parenting style makes little difference to children is highly con- troversial as it may lead parents to make less effort to provide good environments for children. On a research level, there is a logical flaw in attempting to apply figures showing the influence of genetics on a population to individuals – we simply do not know from twin studies and the like to what extent cognitive ability is due to genes in any individual. Horowitz *et al.* (1990) has explained the same findings by taking an opposite approach, saying that although their genes make some children more resilient to a poor environment than others, for most children it is the environment that determines how they develop.

Molecular genetics and cognitive abilities

Another exciting direction in which behavioural genetics research has moved in the 1990s is towards research in molecular genetics. Technological advances have allowed us to begin to extract genes from people, and to begin to identify certain genes that seem likely to affect specific psychological characteristics. The easiest way to establish that a particular gene may be implicated in affecting a characteristic is to look at whether people who exhibit that characteristic are more likely to have the gene. For example, we know that 40 per cent of people with **Alzheimer's disease**, which severely impairs cognitive abilities, have a mutation in a particular gene called apolipoprotein E, situated in Chromosome 19, as opposed to 15 per cent of the whole population. However, not everyone who has the mutation develops Alzheimer's, and not all Alzheimer's patients have the mutant gene, therefore it seems that this mutation is just one of several risk factors. Other genes and a number of environmental factors are also involved.

As well as the presence of mutations in genes, normal variations within genes may also affect psychological functioning. These variations are called polymorphisms. At the time of writing the search for the forms of genes that affect individual differences in cognitive abilities are at an early stage. However, one recent study does appear to have pinpointed variations in a single gene that account for a small amount of the variance in general cognitive ability between people. Robert Plomin and colleagues at the Institute of Psychiatry in London (Chorney *et al.*, 1998) have discovered that a form of the gene IG2FR occurs more commonly in people with very high IQ than in those of average ability.

KEY STUDY: M.J. Chorney, K. Seese, M.J. Owen, J. Daniels, P. McGuffin, L.A. Thompson, D.K. Detterman, C.P. Benbow, D. Lubinsky, T.C. Eley and R. Plomin (1998) A quantitative trait locus (QTL) associated with cognitive ability in children. *Psychological Science* 9, 159–166.

Aim: The researchers were interested in seeing whether any genetic differences could be found between children of average and very high IQ. The rationale of the study was that any differences in particular genes would point towards those genes being directly involved in cognitive ability.

Method: Two matched groups of children were established. The 'superbright' group were taken from a summer camp run for children with very high IQ by Iowa State University. They were matched against a group of children the same age, but with an average IQ. The median IQ of the 'superbright' group was 136. That of the control group was 103 (the average IQ in the population is exactly 100). The researchers extracted DNA from the cells of members of the two groups and analysed their genetic make-up. The aim of the analysis was to see whether particular genes, mutations or polymorphisms were significantly more common in either the 'superbright' group or the average group.

Results: There was a significant difference between the two groups in the frequency of a single gene, situated on Chromosome 6: 33 per cent of the 'superbrights' as opposed to only 17 per cent of the control group had a particular form of the gene IGF2R. This indicated that one form of IGF2R is associated with very high IQ, and thus that IGF2R is one of the genes associated with cognitive ability. The researchers estimated that IGF2R accounts for about 2 per cent of the variance in intelligence.

Discussion

This study provides clear evidence that there are genetic influences on cognitive ability. In the light of the weaknesses of other research methods, such as twin studies, this is perhaps the most convincing evidence of a genetic basis to intelligence. It is interesting, however, that the form of IGF2R associated with high IQ was present in some of the average group and not in the majority of the 'superbright' group. This means that there are clearly other – perhaps more important – influences on cognitive ability than IGF2R. Although this study is groundbreaking in showing that a gene contributes to cognitive ability, on its own it does not tell us *how* heritable cognitive ability is. Furthermore, like any new finding, results on IGF2R need to be replicated in further studies before we can accept them as hard facts.

At the time of writing, IGF2R is the only gene that has been identified as associated with cognitive ability. However, *intellectual development* is affected by other factors apart from innate cognitive ability. One factor which influences success in school is how easily a child becomes bored. In the gene DRD4 there is a sequence of 48 repeated base pairs. The number of repeats varies from one person to another. Ebstein *et al.* (1995) compared people with more repeats and those with fewer repeats and found that those with more DRD4 repeats tended to be more novelty seeking than people with short DRD4 chains. Since then studies have found that hyperactive children also tend to have more DRD4 repeats than others (LaHoste *et al.*, 1996). Children who are hyperactive or novelty seeking may have a harder time at school and hence not develop to their potential. Of course there are numerous factors affecting a child's ability to concentrate in class, and genes are probably not the most important factor in most children. However, thinking back to Scarr's idea that children evoke certain types of environment according to genetically determined personality characteristics, it might be that DRD4 contributes to the development of individual cognitive abilities by affecting children's evocation of their learning environment.

The molecular genetic studies we have looked at here share one important limitation. They identify which genes are more likely to be present in people with a certain characteristic, but they do not tell us whether those genes are active or not. This means that to a certain extent we are making an informed guess as to whether that gene is involved in a psychological characteristic. A recent breakthrough may change this. Watson and Akil (1999) have described the use of gene chips and gene arrays. These are very new and technically complex. The principle underlying both techniques is that active genes can be identified by labelling them with a fluorescent marker and tracing the marker to chemicals produced by the action of the genes. This approach is set to revolutionise the field of behavioural genetics by showing us directly what genes are active in individuals displaying certain psychological characteristics.

Discussion of behavioural genetics

This is an approach to psychology that arouses strong feelings, and many psychologists are concerned about the moral questions raised by behavioural genetics. These issues are complex. Historically, some very unsavoury political creeds such as the **Eugenics** movement, which advocates selective breeding to improve the human gene-pool, and the Nazis, who tried to eliminate 'inferior' genes by genocide (see Chapter 7 for details), have based their ideas on a crude understanding of genetics. This history has tainted the reputation of behavioural genetics. Certainly, if we had a complete understanding of our genes some awkward social issues would arise. Would we still have equal rights once one person could demonstrate their genetic superiority over another? How would human society change once we could produce perfect designer babies? What would become of the abortion debate once we could estimate the potential 'value' of a particular foetus? There is also some concern that an overemphasis on genetic influences on human psychology may lead us to neglect the importance of people's environment for their development.

Whilst these issues are very real, there is also a danger of throwing the genetic baby out with the social bathwater. A modern understanding of genetics tells us that environment is at least as important as genes; thus eugenics would simply not work, and no amount of genetic manipulation would mean that good parenting, healthcare and schooling would cease to be important for children. There *are* ways in which parenting, healthcare and schooling can be *aided* by behavioural genetics, however. Phenylketonuria (PKU) is a genetic condition in which 1 in 10,000 babies do not have the ability to control an amino-acid called phenylalanine, leading to severe mental retardation. By identifying children with PKU at birth, doctors can prevent retardation simply by prescribing a diet low in phenylalanine. As our understanding of both genetics and environment improves, it seems likely that the same principles we currently use to treat PKU will be applied for a range of psychological problems. Say, for example, we found that a particular gene was identified as one of several risk factors for a behavioural or learning difficulty, and that we also knew about environmental risk factors (remember that behavioural geneticists also study environmental factors in development). Children with the high-risk genetic make-up could be targeted at birth and environmental risk factors avoided.

> What do you think about the debates around behavioural genetics? Do the practical applications outweigh the potential problems, and how might we go about tackling these difficulties?

Progress exercise

Evolutionary psychology: the genetics of human similarity

We have already discussed the importance of genes in affecting individual differences between people. However, as we all share 99.9 per cent of our genes, it is also important to look at aspects of our genetic make-up which may influence the behaviours that are common to all of us. We have evolved into humans over millions of years, and it is possible that some aspects of our behaviour have arisen through evolution. **Evolution** has been defined as 'the process by which new species arise as the result of gradual changes to the genetic make-up of existing species over long periods of time' (Clamp and Russell, 1998, p. 1). Darwin's (1859) theory of natural selection states that in each generation of a species not all individuals will survive, and that those which survive and pass on their genes to the next generation are likely to have been better adapted to their environment than those that died. This means that over many generations the genetic make-up of a species changes in ways that make it increasingly well-adapted to its environment.

A classic example of a characteristic that might be explained by natural selection is the long neck of the giraffe. Presumably, as the ancestors of the modern giraffe had to take food from the branches of tall trees, those with the longest necks were best adapted to the environment and so tended to survive. As the individuals with the longest necks in each generation survived and passed on the genes for long necks, over many generations there came to be more and more giraffes with long necks – i.e. the giraffes *evolved* longer and longer necks. The idea behind evolutionary psychology is that, like the giraffe's long neck, some human characteristics and behaviours may have developed through natural selection, and are passed on from one generation to the next through genes. Behaviours and characteristics that increase the ability of an individual to survive and reproduce are known as **adaptive** behaviours or characteristics.

Evolutionary approaches have been applied to many areas in psychology. We can look here at two issues from an evolutionary perspective. It is widely accepted that some aspects of children's abilities and behaviour have been shaped by evolution. More controversial is the idea that some aspects of adult social behaviour, such as mate selection, are also influenced by evolution.

Innate behaviour and abilities in children

One area where we can look for evidence of natural selection is in the abilities and behaviours of babies. From birth, babies will instinctively look for something to suck on, and show a preference for the company of other humans. We know that these are innate rather than learnt behaviours because they are present in all babies and because they are present from birth. From an evolutionary perspective, both of these behaviours are likely to have evolved because they maximise the chances of being fed, and hence surviving to reproduce. Human children, like the young of other mammals, display curious and playful behaviour. From an evolutionary perspective, curiosity and play in childhood are adaptive because they help us learn about the world and develop skills that become useful later.

Humans and other higher mammals have a strong innate need to form attachments to others (see Flanagan, 1999, in this series, for a good account of attachment). Failure to form a secure attachment in childhood has serious psychological consequences. Bowlby (1969) proposed that the instinct to form attachments in infancy has evolved because attachment provides a child with a secure base from which they can explore and to return to for safety when they are threatened. This tendency to remain in proximity to the caregiver and to return to them when threatened is adaptive because it means a caregiver will be on hand to help, and possibly because it makes it harder for predators to take children.

Children are also born with certain abilities. From as soon as nine minutes after birth babies will focus their attention on objects resembling a human face (Goren *et al.*, 1975). At one month of age, the child has difficulty shifting attention from one object to another. Knight and Johnston (1997) observed that at this stage babies frequently burst into tears when shifting attention from one object to another. From an evolutionary perspective, the ability to focus on the caregiver's face is adaptive because it aids the formation of an attachment between infant and caregiver (as we have already established attachment is itself adaptive). It is also possible that the tendency of young babies to cry when switching attention from one thing to another is adaptive because it means that whenever the baby looks at something new the caregiver is alerted and can help the child examine the object that has attracted its attention.

Mate selection

Darwin (1871) suggested that one way in which natural selection takes place is by sexual selection. In many animal species males compete directly for females (for example red deer), and in a few cases females compete for males (for example sea horses). Because males can potentially fertilise large numbers of females and need to invest little time and effort in their part of the reproductive process, their priority is to fertilise a large number of females, choosing their mates on the basis of their availability and fertility. Females on the other hand invest far more in reproduction, therefore they have more to lose if they choose a poor mate. Furthermore, being a scarce resource they can be selective about their mates.

Evolutionary psychologists have used these ideas to explain some aspects of human mating behaviour. Some people have observed for example that men tend to be more promiscuous and less choosy than women. In one recent survey of students' sexual habits, for example, Buss and Schmidt (1993) found that males wanted more sexual partners, expected sex after knowing someone a shorter time and were less fussy about who they slept with as compared to females. Archer (1996) has suggested that further support for the idea of greater promiscuity in men comes from comparing gay male, lesbian and heterosexual relationships. According to Archer, lesbians are less promiscuous and form more stable relationships than heterosexuals, whereas gay men, at least prior to the advent of AIDS, tended to be more promiscuous and form less stable relationships than hetero-sexuals.

It has also been observed that men tend to value youth and physical attractiveness highly, whereas women tend to put more of a premium on signs of wealth and status. Buss (1995) looked at studies of mate selection across a range of cultures and concluded that this tendency is common to all human cultures. In evolutionary terms this makes sense because, in order to maximise the probability of reproduction, males should seek females who are young and healthy (hence best able to bear children). Females, on the other hand, can maximise the probability of reproducing and their child being well cared for by choosing an older, wealthy man who is in a good position to provide materially for her and the child.

Discussion of evolutionary psychology

It is now widely agreed that we are not born a blank slate, as the early behaviourists believed. Given that all humans are born with certain abilities and behaviours, evolutionary psychology provides a credible explanation of the origins of these abilities and behaviours. Given also that we believe that much behaviour in other species is a product of evolution, it would be rather arrogant to assume that we alone have escaped the influence of evolution on our behaviour.

Although there is nothing particularly controversial about applying evolutionary ideas to infant abilities and behaviour, looking at adult social behaviour in evolutionary terms is a different matter. In Chapter 7 we looked at the idea that popular discourse can construct ideas of what is 'masculine' and 'feminine'. Social constructionist and feminist writers have pointed out that popular stereotypes of male and female behaviour are likely to have been socially constructed for the benefit of men rather than evolved. Clearly, the idea that men are naturally *meant* to be promiscuous but that women are not puts men in a position to 'have their cake and eat it', while women have both to put up with promiscuous men and place restrictions on their own sex lives!

Logic also dictates that evolution cannot account for *all* aspects of our social behaviour. A purely evolutionary approach would, for example, find it difficult to explain why the sexual tastes of many people diverge so far from the practices that would maximise the probability of successful reproduction. Not all men seek women of optimum child-bearing age, nor do all women seek out older high-status men for material gain. If, reading this, you find that kind of stereotyping insulting you are far from alone!

Looking at mate selection and sexual behaviour as an example, you can see that although evolution may be one factor influencing our social behaviour it is certainly not the only one. We also learn behaviour from others and take on board the norms and values of a culture. Buss's research notwithstanding, there is also considerable cultural variation in mating habits. The psychodynamic study of relationships has shown that our own family background influences the choices we make about our own relationships. Social constructionism teaches us that we also need to be wary about taking ideas concerning the nature of men and women at face value. Finally, being able to think about these issues, we probably have a degree of free will (as emphasised by humanistic psychologists), and can make conscious choices about our social behaviour rather than simply responding to instinct.

Contemporary issue: does behavioural genetics pose a threat to other psychological approaches?

Looking for the first time at the powerful evidence for genetic influences on behaviour we might be tempted to say that other psychological approaches, particularly those which focus on aspects of the environment, have been rendered obsolete. Certainly, this view has become common in the literature of popular science, and may have a lot to do with the wariness with which many psychologists regard behavioural genetics.

There are, however, two major reasons why behavioural genetics can be integrated into psychology without threat to other approaches. First, behavioural geneticists do not generally claim that all or even most individual differences can be explained by genetics alone. The environment will always be important, and the study of learning and psychodynamics continues to provide information about how the environment impacts on the individual. Second, other psychological approaches frequently seek to answer quite different questions from those examined by behavioural geneticists. Thus, whilst social constructionists are probably correct to point out the constructed nature of, and the dangers in, the concept of 'intelligence', this is an entirely separate research agenda from that of behavioural geneticists who examine the origins of cognitive ability. Similarly, even if behavioural geneticists discovered genetic influences on people's abilities to be good parents (they have!), this does not take anything away from the emotional significance of good parenting for children's development as studied in the field of psychodynamic psychology.

Contributions and limitations of genetically based approaches

Both behavioural genetics and evolutionary psychology are currently very popular in psychology. They have made the following contributions to our understanding of human nature.

- An understanding of genetics has shown us that we are not infinitely adaptable in response to our environment, but rather that some aspects of both human nature in general and individual differences between people are fixed and due to our biology.
- Evolutionary psychology has given us a new angle to explore when investigating a psychological phenomenon – why might this behaviour or ability be particularly useful to us now or have been in our evolutionary past? It has thus enhanced our understanding of numerous areas in psychology, for example attachment and infant behaviour.
- Behavioural genetics has practical applications, such as screening for PKU, and as our understanding of genetics increases the range of these applications will probably increase.

However, despite these contributions there are limitations and controversies surrounding biological approaches to psychology:

- Genetically based approaches can be guilty of reductionism – i.e. they reduce complex psychological phenomena to simple biological processes. Richardson (1997) has compared the role of genes in affecting behaviour to that of wheel nuts affecting the behaviour of buses – they are necessary and we can soon see when they are missing or defective, but genes do not *determine* behaviour anymore than wheel nuts determine bus routes.

- There are risks of social irresponsibility in these approaches. Over-emphasising the impact of genetic factors in the social or intellectual development of children can potentially lead to neglect of the importance of providing children with a good environment. Scientists who speak of genes controlling or determining psychological factors are exaggerating the importance of genetic factors and underplaying the role of the environment. Similarly, over-emphasising the evolutionary influences on human behaviour can stifle social change and foster an amoral 'survival of the fittest' mentality.

- Because biological approaches to psychology draw upon very scientific ideas it is very easy to fall into the trap of seeing them as more respectable than 'soft' approaches to psychology like the psychodynamic approach. However, there is considerable speculation involved in some biological aspects of psychology. There is for example little *direct* evidence for the role of evolution in affecting our behaviour.

Summary

Genes may be important in influencing human behaviour in two major ways. The field of behavioural genetics is concerned with the heritability of psychological characteristics and looks to explain individual differences between people. One important area of study is intelligence or cognitive ability. Twin studies have shown that genetically identical twins are more similar in their cognitive ability, as measured by IQ tests, than genetically non-identical fraternal twins. This implies that genes play a role in affecting individual cognitive ability. More recently, a study found that a particular form of the gene IGF2R is much more common in children with very high IQs, providing more direct support for the idea of a role for genes in cognitive ability. Evolutionary psychology is concerned with the role our genetic make-up may play in affecting the behaviours common to all of us. It is generally accepted that infants have acquired certain characteristics and abilities by evolution. More controversial is the idea that we are affected in our adult social behaviour by evolution.

Review exercise

Look back at the three vignettes in Chapter 1. Now that you know a little more about genetics and genetic influences on psychology, reflect on how well behavioural genetics and evolutionary psychology explain each of these scenarios. You may find it helpful to note down what aspects of each situation a genetic approach can explain fully, and where it runs into some difficulties.

Further reading

Clamp, A. and Russell, J. (1998) *Comparative Psychology*, London: Hodder & Stoughton. Contains very readable chapters on evolution and the evolution of human behaviour.

Plomin, R., DeFries, J.C., McClearn, G.E. and Rutter, M. (1997) *Behavioural Genetics*, New York: Freeman. A clear and detailed state-of-the-art account of the field of behavioural genetics.

Tavris, C. and Wade, C. (1997) *Psychology in Perspective*, New York: Longman. Excellent information on both evolutionary psychology and behavioural genetics.

9

Biological psychology 2: neurophysiology

Key assumptions of the approach

If you have studied biology, you may by now be asking some very reasonable questions about the relationship between biology and psychology. Surely there must be biological influences on psychology, yet rather surprisingly it is quite possible to read most of a psychology textbook like this without a mention of the humble brain. Regardless of other factors, all thinking, feeling and behaviour is ultimately dependent on the brain and the rest of the nervous system. In this chapter we shall look very briefly at the structure and function of the brain, and at some of the techniques we use to study it. We can then look in depth at bodily rhythms, sleep and dreams, and examine a key application of this field – understanding the effects of shiftwork and jet lag. We can then have a look at a contemporary issue in psychology: whether differences in the abilities and characteristics of men and women can be explained by biological differences. First, however, let us look at the assumptions that underlie the neurophysiological approach to psychology:

- *Like other biological approaches to psychology, neurophysiology is a science.* It uses advanced technology to monitor what is happening in the brain, the rest of the nervous system and other body systems and link these to psychological function.
- *Whereas behavioural psychology is most concerned with observable behaviour, psychodynamic psychology with emotion and cognitive psychology with thinking, neurophysiology is concerned primarily with physiological activity.* This can include activation of a particular area of the brain, a change in hormone levels, or a change in the brain's electrical output.
- *Neurophysiology emphasises the importance of physiological processes in affecting behaviour, thinking and feelings.* Thus a physiological approach to depression would emphasise the importance of alterations to levels of chemicals like serotonin in the brain which are typical of depression.

The brain

Although in some ways the brain is still a mystery to psychologists, we do now have some knowledge about the brain's structure and functioning. A fuller account of the working of the nervous system and the ways in which this impacts on human behaviour can be found in John Stirling's *Cortical Functions* and Kevin Silber's *The Physiological Basis of Behaviour: Neural and Hormonal Processes* (both in this series). For now, though, we can have a brief look at the structure and function of the brain.

Looking at Figure 9.1 we can pick out a few of the major parts of the brain and examine what we know of their functions. The fact that different parts of the brain are involved in particular functions is known as **functional localisation**.

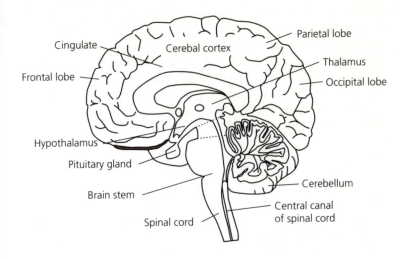

Figure 9.1 **Sagittal section through the human brain**

The brain stem is the point at which the spinal cord enters the brain. In the brain stem is the medulla, which contains all the nerve fibres that connect the brain to the body via the spinal cord. It also contains centres involved in vital functions such as breathing and heartbeat. Major damage to the medulla is thus instantly fatal.

The cerebellum

This is a small area resembling the larger brain cortex. It is situated at the lower back of the brain and is believed to be involved in the motor system, being particularly important in walking. Damage to the cerebellum may cause disruption to the person's ability to walk or muscular weakness in the limbs in general, but few other symptoms.

The diencephalon

This is in the centre of the brain, and consists of two structures, the thalamus and hypothalamus. The hypothalamus seems to play a role in monitoring the state of the body and organising responses. For example, if we are hungry the hypothalamus probably plays a role in motivating us to eat. Rats whose hypothalami have been deliberately damaged respond with abnormal eating behaviour. The thalamus is a relay station which takes information and relays it to the necessary parts of the brain. For example, information about a loud noise is relayed from the auditory cortex, which processes sound, to the amygdala, which plays a role in emotional responses. Thus a response of fear is generated in response to the sound.

The temporal lobes

These are situated at the bottom of the brain and contain a number of structures including the amygdala and the hippocampus. Although psychologists do not have a detailed knowledge of how these operate, we know that they play some role in memory. In Chapter 5 we looked at the case of HM, who had severe damage done to his temporal lobes following an operation, and who has since been unable to store new memories. We also believe that the temporal lobes – in particular the amygdala – play a role in emotion. LeDoux (1993) has proposed that the amygdala functions as an emotional computer that analyses sensory information and triggers the correct response. Damage to the temporal lobes can produce distinctive emotional responses, ranging from heightened emotion and aggression to dependence and passivity. The auditory cortex is also situated in the temporal lobes.

The frontal lobes

The frontal lobes, situated behind the eyes, are important in higher mental functions. They are the main site of thinking, reasoning, analysing and planning. Damage to the frontal lobes can result in personality change and reduced ability to think and reason. Short-term memory function is also based at least partially in the frontal lobes. At the back of the frontal lobes on each side are situated the motor cortices. These control all the voluntary muscles of the body. Each motor cortex controls the opposite side of the body, thus damage to the left motor cortex – common in strokes – leaves the right side of the body partially or completely paralysed.

Discussion of localisation of brain function

Looking at this small selection of brain structures you can see how they impact on our thinking, emotion and behaviour. Thinking depends on the functioning of the frontal lobes, memory and emotion on the frontal and temporal lobes. For movement we rely on the frontal lobes and the cerebellum. In order to regulate our behaviour in response to the needs of the body we rely on the diencephalon. Knowing that certain parts of the brain are involved in psychological functions is interesting and has practical applications – for example, in predicting the effects of brain surgery on the psychological functioning of the patient. Just as we have done here for brain structure, we could look for associations between brain chemistry and behaviour, and gain an insight into the chemical basis of psychological functioning.

However, this approach does not necessarily answer the sort of questions psychologists want answered. Interesting as neurophysiology is in its own right it is only really relevant to psychologists if it can tell us something about how psychological phenomena occur, as well as where they occur. For example, knowing that damage to the temporal lobes can have severe effects on human memory does not tell us how long-term memory works or why most of us forget things. Knowing that the amygdala is important in emotion does not in itself make us feel better! One reason why our knowledge of brain physiology and its relationship to psychological functioning is so limited is that our methods of studying the brain are quite primitive in relation to the complexity of brain function. Before we go any further, let us look briefly at some of the major methods for studying the functioning of the brain.

Techniques for measuring brain function

Imaging techniques

Commonly known as brain scans, there are a variety of techniques which produce images, either on film or on a TV monitor, of the structure or function of the brain. Structural imaging techniques include computerised axial tomography (CAT) and magnetic resonance imaging (MRI). These produce images of sections of the brain. These look rather as if we have cut through the brain and taken a photograph.

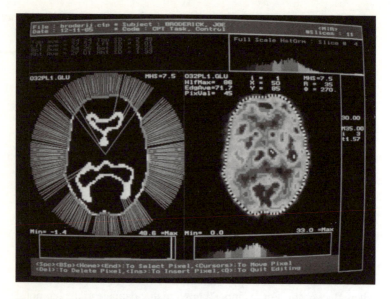

Figure 9.2 **An example of a PET scan, reproduced by permission of Art Directors & TRIP Photo Library**

CAT and MRI work in different ways. CAT scans take x-ray photographs from many angles and these images are then assembled into a single image by a computer. MRI uses a powerful magnetic field instead of x-rays to produce a series of images that are similarly assembled by computer into one image. MRI is capable of producing much clearer images than CAT. MRI and CAT are of some value to psychologists because they allow us to compare the structure of brains that are functioning normally and abnormally and hence help to establish whether a physical abnormality is responsible for a symptom.

Functional imaging techniques allow us to see a little of what is actually happening in the brain, hence they are often more useful to psychologists. Positron emission tomography (PET) scanning involves injecting oxygen or glucose carrying a positron-emitting radioactive label. (An example of a PET scan is shown in Figure 9.2) This ceases to be radioactive fairly quickly and so does no harm to the participant. What it means, however, is that by measuring the radiation levels in different parts of the brain we can gain a good idea of which part is using the most oxygen and glucose. If the participant is performing a particular task at the time, this tells us what parts of the brain are involved in the task. In Chapter 5 we looked at face recognition. A PET study by Haxby *et al.* (1991) showed that when participants were given a task involving matching pairs of faces or sets of dots different areas of the brain were active. This shows us that the brain's mechanisms for face recognition are different from those of ordinary object recognition.

PET scanning has the problem that many tasks cannot easily be performed whilst in a scanner. One way around this is to use SPET (single photon emission tomography). This also involves a radioactive isotope entering the blood, usually Tc-hexamethylpropyleneamine oxime (fortunately we can shorten this to HMPAO!), but the crucial difference is that once HMPAO enters brain tissue it becomes trapped for some time. We can thus give someone a task in a suitable environment and scan them later. This is especially useful for studying autistic children, who cannot be scanned without sedation and hence could not otherwise be scanned performing particular tasks (Springer and Deutsch, 1998).

The final major approach to functional imaging is fMRI (functional magnetic resonance imaging). Like structural MRI, fMRI involves generating a powerful magnetic field around the head. Because blood carrying oxygen has different magnetic properties from blood carrying deoxygenated blood, taking several MRI scans in sequence can identify where blood is flowing to in the brain, and hence what regions of the brain are particularly active. fMRI is particularly useful for observing the sequence of brain areas activated in tasks. In one recent fMRI study Eden *et al.* (1996) compared the sequence of brain activation in dyslexic and non-dyslexic children when reading. They found that the dyslexic children were not activating a particular part of the brain (called the posterior visual cortex) when they read. fMRI has been growing in importance in recent years but it has its drawbacks, one being that the slightest movement by the participant can ruin a scan.

EEG and MEG

The EEG (electroencephalograph) literally means 'electric brain writing'. Because brain activity involves transmission of electric impulses from one cell to the next, monitoring this electric activity can give us clues as to what is taking place in the brain. In humans this is normally done by placing electrodes on the scalp, although in some situations such as during brain surgery electrodes may be placed inside the brain. The patterns of electrical activity picked up by EEG are called brain waves. There are four major types of brain waves, distinguished by their frequency (i.e. how often they occur). Frequency is measured in hertz (Hz), which means the number of times the wave occurs in one second. These are shown below:

- Delta waves have a frequency of 1–3 Hz. These are most commonly seen in deep sleep.
- Theta waves have a frequency of 4–7 Hz. In adults these are normally only seen in those suffering from psychopathic personality disorder.
- Alpha waves have a frequency of 8–12 Hz. These are most common in awake and relaxed adults.
- Beta waves have a frequency of 13Hz+. These are most common in adults who are alert and concentrating on something.

Measuring brainwaves has had a number of useful applications in psychology and has become increasingly sophisticated. Gevins *et al.* (1995) placed 125 electrodes on the scalp of a participant and connected these to a computer while the participant performed various cognitive tasks. By analysing the electrical activity in different parts of the brain during each task, the computer produced information about the sequence in which different regions were active during each cognitive task. This type of research provides useful information to go along with imaging studies.

Despite the usefulness of EEG, it will always be limited by the fact that what we can measure on the scalp reflects the electrical activity of a huge number of brain cells working together. It is not sensitive enough to record the activity of smaller groups of cells. Furthermore, EEG only gives a rough idea of where the activated brain cells are. To get around these difficulties the MEG or magnetoencephalogram has been developed. Rather than measuring the traces of electricity that travel from active brain cells to the scalp, MEG measures the magnetic fields created by groups of brain cells working together. Unlike electrical signals, magnetic fields are not disrupted by passing through the skull, hence MEG gives much more precise readings of the strength and location of brain cell activity than EEG. The major difficulty with

MEG is that the tiny magnetic fields it measures are easily disrupted by other magnetic sources. At the time of writing MEG is still being perfected, but it has already yielded some fascinating results that could not easily have been obtained by other means.

Lesioning studies

A lesion in the brain is an area of dead tissue. Often we get the chance to study naturally occurring lesions in humans following strokes and other brain injuries. However, relying on naturally occurring lesions has its limitations. Often large areas (or several different areas) of the brain are damaged so we only get to see very approximately what the effects are of damage to a particular region. Also we may have to wait a long time for a patient to come along with precisely the type of lesion we are interested in. The alternative for researchers is to produce their own lesions. Clearly this would be unacceptable in humans, because of the horrendous effects on the participant, but lesioning studies of animals have been carried out.

Lesions are produced in the animal when under anaesthetic by drilling a hole in the skull and using an electric current to burn away a small area of brain. The animal is then carefully observed to see whether any aspects of its behaviour have changed. An early lesioning study was carried out by Hetherington and Ranson (1942). They produced a lesion in part of the hypothalamus of a rat and observed that the rat ate uncontrollably, trebling its normal body weight. This type of study has been invaluable in understanding the role of the hypothalamus in eating behaviour.

Bodily rhythms and sleep

'We live in a rhythmic world. Night follows day, the seasons on Earth and the stars above follow their annual patterns, lawn daisies close at night and open at daylight, pubs open and close!' (Bentley, 1999 in this series, p. 11). Human and animal behaviour follow a number of cycles or **rhythms**. These rhythms are classified according to their time-scale. Circadian rhythms are those that last about a day, ultradian rhythms are those that last less than a day, and infradian rhythms are those which last more than a day. One infradian rhythm in humans is the menstrual cycle, which lasts approximately 28 days. There are numerous ultradian rhythms. One example is cognitive vigilance, which cycles at about an hour and a half, and affects performance on mental tasks. What this means is our cognitive abilities peak and fall off again approximately every 90 minutes.

An example of a circadian rhythm is the sleep–wake cycle. We all know from experience that most of us need to sleep between six and nine hours per night, but that some people need more sleep than others. Margaret Thatcher reportedly needed only a couple of hours sleep a night while she was prime minister. Some less fortunate people need more than the usual six to nine hours. Unfortunately employers are under no legal obligation to let you start work later in the morning if you fall into this category!

It seems that the regulation of the sleep–wake cycle is dependent on both internal and external factors. Within the brain we have at least one **bodyclock** which helps regulate our circadian rhythm. We believe that one bodyclock is situated in a region called the suprachiasmatic nucleus (or SCN). This is near the top of the brain, just where the optic nerves cross. The SCN is shown in Figure 9.3.

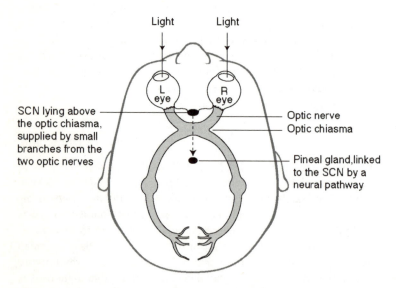

Figure 9.3 **The position of the suprachiasmatic nucleus**

In a recent animal experiment Morgan (1995) demonstrated that the SCN controls the length of the sleep–wake cycle in hamsters. He obtained mutant hamsters whose sleep–wake cycle differed from the usual 24 hours and transplanted their SCNs into the brains of normal hamsters. These formerly normal hamsters quickly took on the circadian rhythm of the mutants. Of course this particular study only shows that the SCN is involved in the circadian rhythm in rodents. However, psychologists tend to believe that the SCN is also important in regulating human circadian rhythms.

The SCN contains nerve cells that fire nerve impulses at regular intervals. We believe that it is this regular firing which maintains the timing of the bodyclock. Although the SCN can keep time on its own it is regularly 'reset' by information from the optic nerves about time of day, based on light and dark. The SCN is connected to the pineal gland, which produces a chemical called melatonin. When there is a build-up of melatonin in the blood we feel sleepy. It is believed that after dark the information from the SCN lets the pineal gland know to produce more melatonin, hence we get tired at night.

We have already seen that the working of the bodyclock is affected by what is happening in the environment. Environmental changes such as dawn and dusk that reset the body's rhythms are called **zeitgebers**. These are important for a number of reasons. There may for example be an evolutionary advantage to sleeping at night in keeping us out of reach of predators, therefore having darkness cue us to sleep is adaptive. As we shall see in a moment the human bodyclock does not actually have a cycle of 24 hours unless it is reset regularly by zeitgebers. If we are to function on a planet with a 24-hour day we need a zeitgeber such as daylight to give us a regular sleep–wake cycle. In a classic study one man removed himself from all zeitgebers and found that his bodyclock had a cycle slightly longer than 24 hours. In 1972 a French geologist called Siffre spent seven months underground. He had food and equipment and a telephone to connect him to the outside world. He had, however, no means of knowing the time. Siffre continued to have a regular sleep–wake cycle, but it altered from 24 hours to 25. A more recent study looked at a woman who, when all zeitgebers were removed, revealed a 30-hour circadian rhythm. We can look at this study in detail.

KEY STUDY: S. Folkard (1996) Bags of time to play. *Daily Express*, 28 September.

Aim: The researchers were interested in the effects on a female volunteer of being deprived of all zeitgebers. As well as looking at the time of the sleep–wake cycle this study focused on the participant's perception of time and measured her daily cycle of body temperature change.

Method: This was a single-participant experiment in which a volunteer participant (a university student called Kate Aldcroft) was selected and placed in the controlled environment of a psychology laboratory for 25 days. During this time she had no access to any zeitgebers. She could see no daylight and had no access to clocks or any other sources of information about time such as television. The times at which she woke and slept were noted, and her body temperature was recorded several times a day. In order to gain a measure of the participant's subjective perception of time she was asked to play *Amazing Grace* on the bagpipes twice a day at what she believed to be the same time.

Results: The participant's temperature continued to cycle at 24 hours in the absence of zeitgebers. Interestingly, however, her sleep–wake cycle altered to around 30 hours, with periods of sleep as long as 16 hours being recorded. Aldcroft's subjective perception of time proved inaccurate, and she played the bagpipes at times differing each day by several hours.

Discussion

These results tell us several interesting things. First, it appears that the body's temperature cycle operates on a 24-hour basis and is not dependent on zeitgebers. Second, the sleep–wake cycle *does* appear to require zeitgebers to remain at 24 hours. It is particularly interesting to note that this participant had a cycle of 30 hours, as opposed to the 25 hours of Siffre, implying that there might be wide individual differences in the length of our sleep–wake cycles. Finally this study shows that people (at least this participant) found it very difficult to estimate the time in the absence of zeitgebers. However fascinating the results of this study, it has its limitations. Only one participant was looked at, and the obvious question arises as to how people in general would get on in these circumstances.

The sleep cycle

The sleep cycle is an example of an ultradian rhythm. We sleep in a distinct cycle lasting about 90 minutes which is repeated throughout the night. There are four stages to each cycle of passive sleep and a period of intense brain activity called active sleep:

- *Stage 1 sleep*: this lasts up to 15 minutes as we are falling asleep. The sleeper has a slow heart rate and can easily be wakened.
- *Stage 2 sleep*: this is deeper than stage 1 but people can still be awakened fairly easily.
- *Stage 3 sleep*: the sleeper has a lowered body temperature and blood pressure. They are now difficult to wake.
- *Stage 4 sleep*: this is the deepest level of sleep. The brain is at its least active and the sleeper is very difficult to wake.

Once the sleeper has been in stage 4 for a time the cycle reverses and they go through stages 3, 2 and 1. The person then enters active sleep. This is also called REM sleep because it is characterised by rapid eye movements (REMs). Stages 1–4 are collectively called nREM sleep. REM sleep is when most of our dreams occur, and also when our dreams are longest, most memorable and most vivid. Natural waking occurs most commonly from REM sleep. The dreams we remember are generally those we have during the period of REM from which we wake up. People who say they don't dream are those who tend to wake up from nREM sleep. REM sleep is interesting because EEG reveals that the brain is extremely active, showing similar patterns to the waking state. While in REM sleep the brain becomes highly active, and EEGs show similar patterns to a waking state. Interestingly, although the brain is highly active, people are harder to wake from REM sleep than quiet sleep. Now that we have looked at the basics of sleep, it is worth looking at theories of *why* we sleep and *why* we dream.

Theories of sleep

Restoration theories

Oswald (1976) proposed that sleep has a restorative function. This means that we need a regular period of inactivity in order to somehow 'recharge our batteries'. Certain repair and maintenance jobs on the body, and the brain in particular, can perhaps not be done while we are active. Oswald suggested that adenosine triphosphate (ATP) – the source of energy for the cells that make up our bodies – can only build up in cells during sleep. This may be especially important for the brain, which uses up 20 per cent of the body's energy. According to Oswald's approach sleep allows brain cells to recover after the frantic activity of a day.

Sleep appears to have other restorative functions. Certain essential chemicals are only produced during deep sleep. One such is growth hormone. If you were ever told as a child to go to bed because you only grow in your sleep, and are now a successful basketball player, thank your parents! Growth hormone is also important in protein synthesis, which is needed for the upkeep and repair of all body systems, including the brain. It seems likely therefore that upkeep of the brain requires regular sleep. Maurice (1998) has suggested a third restorative function of sleep. The eye movements of REM sleep help to circulate the fluid in the eyes, allowing oxygen to reach all parts of the eye. Maurice proposed that without REMs the eye would suffer oxygen starvation.

Sleep also seems to be necessary for the production of neurotransmitters, the chemicals that cross between brain cells allowing them to communicate. Although the mechanisms are not well understood, it appears that there is a link between REM sleep and noradrenaline production, and between nREM sleep and the production of serotonin. These neurotransmitters are important in our emotional state, and disruption to them may go some way to explaining why we become less emotionally stable when we have not had enough sleep.

Evaluation of restoration theories

We know that protein synthesis does occur during sleep, and that this is necessary for maintaining all the body's systems, including the brain. Furthermore, athletes in training, babies and those who have recently suffered brain damage – all of whom have a greater need for protein synthesis – tend to sleep more than the rest of us. There is therefore substantial support for the idea that we are somehow replenished by sleep, and that this process involves protein synthesis. However, there are also difficulties with the idea of restoration as a complete explanation of sleep. The body's stores of amino acids, which are needed for protein synthesis, would not last for the eight hours we typically sleep. Therefore we would not expect much protein synthesis to have occurred by morning. A particular difficulty with Maurice's ideas about restoration is that people deprived of sleep are no more likely than anyone else to develop eye problems, thus REMs do not actually appear to be necessary for oxygen transport in the eye. Furthermore, restoration does not explain why we generally prefer to sleep at night rather than in the day. Despite these limitations most psychologists do agree that restoration is *one* important function of sleep, although perhaps not the only one.

Evolutionary theory

Meddis (1975) has proposed that sleep is adaptive to many species because it keeps them out of harm's way at night when they are most vulnerable to predators. Humans have inherited this tendency for sleep from our forebears. Of course it can still be very dangerous to be out and about at night, so sleeping at night is to some extent still adaptive. By contrast to humans and other primates, predators such as cats and owls are nocturnal – i.e. they sleep by day and are active at night. From an evolutionary perspective this may be because prey is most vulnerable at night. If we see humans as prey rather than predator (of course we can be both) then it is important to be quiet and immobile at times when predators are most active.

Looking at a range of animal species we can see that sleeping habits do seem to vary in accordance with their needs. Thus grazing animals such as antelope sleep very little because their predators are active both in the day and at night, and because in their natural environment they can be spotted easily from a distance. By contrast lions (which, at least until humans with guns appeared, had no predators) sleep at any time of day.

Evaluation of evolutionary theory

Meddis's approach is perhaps most useful in explaining *when* we sleep rather than *why*. Certainly looking at a range of animal species we can say that in general each species has evolved the sleep pattern that suits its needs best. However, we can probably not explain why all animals need to sleep in the first place just by reference to evolution. Surely it would be more efficient from an evolutionary perspective for species who are in constant danger not to sleep at all. Yet all animals sleep. Porpoises in the Indus river, which are in constant peril from heavy objects being carried downstream, sleep for a few seconds at a time, but cannot do without sleep altogether.

There are other problems with adopting an evolutionary approach to sleep. If we have evolved sleep in order to keep us quiet and out of danger then we would expect to be rather stiller and quieter whilst asleep than is actually the case. We would expect evolution to have taken care of snoring by now! Furthermore, an evolutionary approach does not take account of cultural variations in sleep-related behaviour. For example, it is common for people in Southern Europe to take a siesta (a short sleep) in the afternoon then to stay up late at night. Of course it could be argued that this is adaptive because it means that people are inactive at the hottest time of day and active later when it is cooler. However, the fact that this pattern is not the norm in all hot countries shows that cultural variations in sleep patterns are not *just* a response to different environment.

Dreams

We dream mostly although not exclusively in REM sleep. Throughout human history dreams have held a fascination for us, and different cultures have held a variety of beliefs about the nature and significance of dreaming. From a physiological perspective, one of the most fundamental and interesting questions about dreams is whether REMs correspond to the content of dreams. Another commonly asked question is whether we dream in real-time. Both these questions were addressed in a classic early study by Dement and Kleitman (1957).

KEY STUDY: W. Dement and N. Kleitman (1957) The relation of eye movements during sleep to dream activity: an objective method for the study of dreaming. *Journal of Experimental Psychology* **53 (5), 339–346.**

Aim: The primary aim of the study was to see whether there was a relationship between REMs and the content of dreams. A secondary aim was to establish whether dreams take place in real-time, or whether they are condensed.

Method: Seven adult participants took part in the study – five males and two females. Each participant reported to the laboratory just before their usual bedtime. They had not consumed alcohol or coffee as these reduce REM sleep. Electrodes were attached near the eyes to measure eye movements and others were attached to the scalp in order to determine the stage of sleep. Each participant then went to bed in a dark, quiet room. An EEG was run for the entire period of sleep. At various times during the night the participants were wakened by means of a loud doorbell, both from REM and nREM sleep. Their task was to describe the nature of their most recent dream into a tape recorder. They were then allowed to return to sleep. The participants were given no feedback about what period of sleep they had been awakened from. In order to see how closely the REMs corresponded with dream content the participants were woken a total of 35 times following distinctive eye movements. The researchers examined the accounts of dreams and the recordings of brain and eye activity, and looked for associations.

Results: REMs occurred regularly in a 90-minute cycle. Far more dreams were reported when participants were woken from REM sleep than nREM sleep. There was a significant correlation between the length of REMs and the length of the dream as reported by the participant. Participants were generally accurate in estimating the length of their dream. This showed that the dreams were experienced in real-time. Most interestingly there was a close association between the distinctive eye movements noted and the content of dreams. For example, one participant had been seen to have only vertical move-ments (as in looking up and down), and their dream was of climbing up and down ladders. Another had a minute of very little eye movement followed by several large movements to the left. Their dream was of driving down the street and being crashed into by a car coming from the left.

Discussion

The results do clearly indicate that people dream in real-time, and that their REMs do relate to the content of their dreams. What has been the subject of some controversy, however, is the most basic finding of this study, and a common assumption: that dreams take place more often in REM sleep than in nREM sleep. Beaumont (1988) has suggested that the reason most participants woken from nREM sleep did not report dreams is not because they occur less than in REM sleep but rather because we find it harder to remember them when waking from nREM sleep.

In Chapter 3 we looked at Freud's theory of dreams, which saw dreaming as having functions of symbolically fulfilling our wishes and helping us to deal with traumatic events. An interesting alternative way of looking at dreaming dreams comes from the physiological approach of Hobson and McCarley in their activation–synthesis theory.

Activation–synthesis theory of dreaming

Hobson and McCarley (1977) proposed that, from a physiological perspective, what we experience as dreams are the result of the brain's attempts to interpret random nerve impulses. In the brain stem (see Figure 9.1) there is an area that, when we are awake, is involved in relaying information from the senses to the brain. As well as letting us know about what is happening around us, this region is responsible for feeding back to us what we ourselves are doing. The idea behind activation–synthesis theory is that when most of the brain is inactive, this region is prone to periodic bursts of random nervous activity. These are picked up and interpreted by other parts of the brain, with the result that we have sensory experiences of being in places and doing things.

There are two distinct stages to the process outlined by Hobson and McCarley. In the *activation stage* the brain stem generates random nerve impulses. The brain stem is a primitive part of the brain unconcerned with thought or emotion, so it appears that the reasons for its activation are physiological rather than psychological. The activation begun in the brain stem spreads to other parts of the brain until it reaches areas of the cortex responsible for higher mental functions. These begin to interpret the information from the brain stem as they would if the dreamer is awake. In the second stage, *synthesis*, the brain produces the dream – i.e. the succession of images and sensations actually experienced by the dreamer by putting together the interpretation of the transmissions from the brain stem and any memories and emotions activated by these. According to Hobson and McCarley the reason why dreams often contain such bizarre and dis-jointed images is because of the difficulty the brain has in synthesising a coherent story from a random series of nerve impulses.

The activation synthesis theory of dreaming has often been used to try to discredit psychodynamic approaches. It is worth looking at what the implications of activation–synthesis really are for the psycho-dynamic idea of dream interpretation. The first point to make is that whereas a physiological approach aims to see what *causes* dreaming in general, the psychodynamic approach is more concerned with the *meaning* of individual dreams and their *psychological functions*. These two very different approaches to explaining dreaming may therefore not actually be incompatible. Hobson (1989) has addressed this issue. He proposed that, in contrast to Freud's ideas, dreams are generated by physiological rather than psychological mechanisms, and there is no evidence that the synthesis process involves disguising latent content in manifest content. However, Hobson has fully supported the central psychodynamic assumption that dreams can reveal much about the conscious and unconscious mind of the dreamer. The synthesis process invokes the memories and emotions of the individual, hence the content of the dream will be highly personal and may reveal a lot about the dreamer's anxieties and wishes. The activation–synthesis model is thus quite compatible with the contemporary psychodynamic idea of dream interpretation.

Evaluation of activation–synthesis theory

As an explanation of how dreams are produced on a physiological level, Hobson and McCarley's approach is highly credible. Support for the idea that we synthesise dreams using whatever information is available to us at the time comes from the fact that we tend to incorporate external events into our dreams if we can perceive them while dreaming. In one early study, for example, Dement and Wolpert (1958) sprinkled water on the faces of sleepers in REM sleep and then woke them. The majority of dreamers had incorporated water into their dream.

There are, however, difficulties with the approach as a complete explanation of dreaming. It cannot easily explain why we *need* REM sleep, nor why people deprived of REM sleep have a 'rebound effect' – i.e. when allowed to sleep normally they have longer periods of REM to make up for that they have missed. Activation–synthesis also runs into problems when explaining why we also have dreams in quiet sleep, although less frequently and less vividly than in REM sleep.

Key application: understanding the effects of shiftwork and jet lag

In our discussion of bodily rhythms up to now we have assumed that people are allowed to sleep when they feel like it, and that zeitgebers always follow regular, natural patterns. Unfortunately this is not always so. In the cases of shiftwork and jet lag we expose ourselves to zeitgebers ranging from unusual meal-times to seeing the sun rise only a few hours after it last rose. This can have serious effects on the body's natural rhythms.

Shiftwork

Many industries and services require people to work 24 hours a day. We would be none too chuffed if we turned up to the casualty department of our local hospital in the middle of the night and were told to come back the next day when the doctors and nurses were awake! The private sector frequently requires people to work through the night, either to meet demand for a product or because equipment needs to be left on and monitored. Shiftworkers are those who work these unsociable hours. Some shiftworkers work a regular but unusual shift, for example at night. Others work irregular shifts, and this can cause more serious problems.

One simple problem with shiftwork is that shiftworkers tend to sleep between one and four hours less per night than others (Akerstedt, 1985). A further problem is that different zeitgebers can be in conflict with one another. Say, for example, your alarm clock goes off at 5 p.m. This is a zeitgeber which tells you (unless you have done shiftwork for many years) that it is morning. However, depending on the time of year, you are likely to encounter dusk then darkness soon after the alarm goes off. This second zeitgeber is in conflict with the first. It seems possible that different zeitgebers set different bodily rhythms, so that when we perceive contradictory zeitgebers in this way we put different bodily rhythms out of sync with one another.

Shiftwork is associated with performance deficits. Novak *et al.* (1990) compared the number of accidents during day and night shifts in a chemical plant and found significantly more accidents at night. Working at night is often associated with feeling sleepy. Studies have shown that when people feel sleepy whilst working at night this is not just a subjective experience – their brain waves are changing. Keckland and Akerstedt (1993) took EEG readings of lorry drivers on 10–12 hour night-time journeys in Sweden. They found that at the times drivers reported themselves to be most sleepy their EEG showed an increase in Alpha and Theta waves, which indicate a decrease in alertness. The lesson from this is clear. When you feel sleepy, for example when driving at night, you are actually less alert and hence at greater risk of an accident. The only answer is to get some sleep. Temporary measures, such as drinking coffee, provide only very short-term relief from sleepiness.

Suggest ways in which (a) the manager of a football team playing abroad and (b) a factory night-manager could reduce the risk of serious performance deficits.

Progress exercise

Jet lag

When we travel long distances from east to west, or vice versa, we cross time zones. This means that we encounter a range of zeitgebers that would reset the bodyclock, perhaps more than once in a journey. Travelling from west to east produces more severe effects than travelling from east to west. This indicates that making our bodyclock skip ahead in time is more disruptive than putting the body-clock behind. In other words it is easier to stay up longer until the bodyclock adapts to the new time zone than it is to sleep prematurely.

Like shiftwork, jet lag is associated with performance deficits, particularly in west–east travel. Schwartz *et al.* (1995) looked at the scores of American baseball teams travelling east and west across the USA for matches. They found that west coast teams travelling east had less than a third of the wins of east coast teams travelling west, confirming that it is harder to adjust to travelling east. Performance deficits associated with jet lag are generally less severe than those associated with shiftwork.

When we look at the effects of jet lag we need to keep in mind a further variable – stress. Travelling is itself stressful, and this stress appears to compound the effects of jet lag. Animal research has shown that stress interferes with the brain's attempts to reset bodily rhythms. Stewart and Amir (1998) compared stressed and non-stressed rats in their ability to use zeitgebers to reset the bodyclock, and found that the stressed rats had more difficulty in adapting to the zeitgebers. If these results can be applied to humans they imply that people who are stressed by travelling are more likely to suffer jet lag because the stress will interfere on a physiological level with the processes of resetting the bodyclock.

Contemporary issue: are gender differences due to biological factors?

When we use the term 'sex' in psychology, as opposed to 'gender', we are talking about biological differences between men and women. Strictly then we should only talk about 'sex differences' in psychological abilities and characteristics when we are quite sure they are biological in origin. This leaves us with something of a problem, however, as we are not really sure what differences between men and women and between boys and girls are biological in origin, and which are a result of social-psychological factors. Whereas we can be reasonably sure that the reasons why men have deeper voices and greater muscle mass than women are biological, the picture becomes much more confused when we look at *psychological* differences between men and women. Say, for example, we decide that boys are better at mathematical tasks than girls but girls are better at verbal tasks (much, though not all, research has supported these stereotypes). On the one hand this could be a result of sex differences in the brains of boys and girls. It might equally be because boys learn at an early age that it is important to be good at mathematical tasks whereas girls learn to concentrate more on developing verbal abilities.

Recent technological developments have allowed us directly to compare the operation of the brains of men and women. Shaywitz *et al.* (1995) used fMRI to compare activity by different regions of the brain in 19 men and 19 women during a variety of language tasks, which included identifying rhyming words and upper- and lower-case letters, and understanding word meanings. No sex differences in brain function emerged when participants were performing word-meaning tasks, nor did any overall sex difference in ability emerge. However, different regions of the brain were activated during the rhyming task. This indicates that in some ways, males and females do deal differently on a physiological level with some aspects of language.

Assuming that there are physiological differences between brain function in males and females, this alone does not tell us the origins of these differences. There is some evidence that hormone levels are associated with differences in cognitive abilities between men and women. Men are traditionally held to be better at spatial tasks. Kimura (1996) looked at the levels of testosterone (a hormone found in higher levels in men than women and associated with sexual development in men) in women and found that women with high levels of testosterone performed better in spatial tasks. This type of study implies that men and women have different abilities as a function of their differing hormone levels.

Evolutionary psychology has also had an input into the debate about gender differences. Silverman and Eales (1992) proposed the hunter-gatherer theory. This suggests that in our evolutionary history males were more likely to be involved in hunting, which requires spatial abilities, both for tracking and killing prey, and for finding one's way around. Women in hunter-gatherer societies are assumed to have been foragers rather than hunters, and to have required good verbal skills to coordinate efficient foraging activities. Language skills would also be particularly useful for bringing up children.

There is thus a body of biological theory and research to suggest that there are biological differences in some aspects of male and female psychology. However, there are equally powerful arguments for the importance of environmental factors in the development of gender-specific characteristics. Social learning theory (see Chapter 2) suggests that children learn gender-specific behaviour through observation of role models and by reinforcement for 'gender-appropriate' behaviour. A more contemporary theory explaining gender development in psychological rather than biological terms comes from Martin and Halverson (1981), who proposed gender schema theory. This is a cognitive approach suggesting that children acquire a **gender schema**, a unit of memory which contains all the individual's knowledge, beliefs, attitudes and feelings about gender. They then actively seek out information to build up the detail in the schema. Children are aware of their own gender and base their own behaviour on the information in their gender schema. There is ample evidence for both social learning of gender and of gender schemas. Thus we cannot say with certainty to what extent gender is a product of biological sex.

Contributions and limitations of biological approaches

Biological approaches to psychology have grown in influence in recent years. Some of its major contributions are as follows:

- Like genetically based approaches, neurophysiology shows us the limitations that our biology places on human psychological functioning. This enhances our general understanding of human nature.
- On occasion, a biological understanding of psychology can enhance our understanding of a social issue. Needleman *et al.* (1996) gave the example of the effects of lead-containing paint on intellectual development in children. One reason why children from lower socio-economic groups do worse in school and in tests of cognitive ability is that they are much more likely to have been exposed to old paint containing lead. We know from biology that lead causes cognitive deficits.
- Biological psychology has a host of practical applications, ranging from understanding and minimising the effects of shiftwork and jet lag to developing drugs that can be used to treat mental disorder.

However, despite these contributions there are limitations and controversies surrounding biological approaches to psychology:

- Biological approaches can be guilty of reductionism – i.e. they reduce complex psychological phenomena to simple biological processes. This can have negative consequences. In the example given above, for example, whilst old paint might be one contributing factor in the relationship between poverty and intellectual development it certainly isn't the only factor or even the most important one. We could not remove the impact of poverty just by repainting all old properties, and it is dangerous and misleading to suggest that we could.

- There will always be some aspects of psychology that cannot be explained by adopting a physiological approach. For example, we might know that people suffering from depression typically have lowered levels of serotonin, and that we can correct this with drugs. However, this does not tell us why people who lost a parent in early childhood are more likely to suffer depression as an adult. That requires another level of explanation that can be provided by one of the other theoretical approaches.

Summary

Biological approaches to psychology use three key ideas from biology, genetics, evolution and physiology to understand psychology. Behavioural genetics is the study of the heritability of psychological characteristics. Genes have been implicated in a number of psychological variables, including intelligence and some mental disorders. Evolutionary psychologists have suggested that many of our characteristics and abilities have developed through a process of evolution because they are useful to us in some way. Neurophysiology focuses on the structure and function of the brain and nervous system and the ways in which these contribute to psychological functioning. New scanning techniques have allowed us to gain an increasing knowledge of brain function. One area of study in neurophysiology concerns bodily rhythms. Our knowledge of circadian rhythms has allowed us to understand the effects of jet lag and shiftwork. An understanding of ultradian rhythms has enriched our knowledge of sleep and dreaming. Several aspects of biological psychology have caused controversy. One such is the idea that psychological differences between men and women are biological rather than social in origin. Although there is increasing evidence for differences in the functioning of male and female brains, this does not in itself answer the question as to the origins of those differences.

Look back at the vignettes in Chapter 1. Now that you know a little more about the neurophysiological approach to psychology, reflect on how well it explains each of these scenarios. You may find it helpful to note down what aspects of each situation a physiological approach can explain fully, and where it runs into difficulties.

Further reading

Bentley, E. (1999) *Awareness: Biorhythms, Sleep and Dreaming*, London: Routledge. Contains excellent, clear and up-to-date accounts of bodily rhythms, sleep and dreams and the effects of shiftwork and jet lag. Designed to be particularly clear for those new to psychology.

Carlson, N.R. (1998) *The Physiology of Behaviour*, Boston: Allyn & Bacon. A very detailed and up-to-date undergraduate-level text that goes into greater detail about many of the issues discussed in this chapter.

Silber, K. (1999) *The Physiological Basis of Behaviour: Neural and Hormonal Processes*, London: Routledge. An introductory overview of the role of the brain, nervous system and hormones in regulating behaviour.

10

Study aids

IMPROVING YOUR ESSAY-WRITING SKILLS

At this point in the book you have acquired the knowledge necessary to tackle the exam itself. Answering exam questions is a skill which this chapter shows you how to improve. Examiners have some ideas about what goes wrong in exams. Most importantly, students do not provide the kind of evidence the examiner is looking for. A grade C answer is typically accurate and reasonably constructed, but has limited detail and commentary. To lift such an answer to a grade A or B may require no more than fuller detail, better use of material and a coherent organisation. By studying the essay presented in this chapter, and the examiner's comment, you can learn how to turn a barely passing essay into one meriting a much higher grade.

Please note that marks given by the examiner in the practice essay should be used as a guide only and are not definitive. They represent the 'raw marks' given by an AEB examiner. That is, the marks the examiner would give to the examining board based on a total of 24 marks per question broken down into skill A (description) and skill B (evaluation). Tables showing this scheme are in Appendix C of Paul Humphreys' title in this series, *Exam Success in AEB Psychology*. They may not be the marks given on the examination certificate received ultimately by the student because all examining boards are required to use a common standardised system called the Uniform

Mark Scale (UMS), which adjusts all raw scores to a single standard acceptable to all examining boards.

The essay is about the length a student would be able to write in 35–40 minutes (leaving extra time for planning and checking). Following the essay are detailed comments about its strengths and weaknesses. The most common problems to look out for are:

- Failure to answer the actual question set and presenting 'one written during your course'.
- A lack of evaluation, or commentary – many weak essays suffer from this.
- Too much evaluation and not enough description. Description is vital in demonstrating your knowledge and understanding of the selected topic.
- Writing 'everything you know' in the hope that something will get credit. Excellence is displayed through selectivity, and therefore improvements can often be made by *removing* material which is irrelevant to the question set.

For more ideas on how to write good essays you should consult *Exam Success in AEB Psychology* (Paul Humphreys) in this series.

Practice essay

Critically consider the contribution of the behaviourist approach to psychology. (24 marks)
AEB A-level January 1997 module 7, question 1.

Candidate's answer

In this essay I will describe the contributions of the behaviourist approach to psychology and then evaluate it in terms of how successful the explanations have been.

The behaviourists have contributed to a great many ideas in psychology, including theories of aggression, of self, gender and morals, abnormal behaviour and so on. In fact there aren't many areas where they have made no contribution. In all these areas the essential theory that is used is conditioning. Pavlov was the first to describe classical conditioning. Classical conditioning is concerned with how an animal learns a new link between two things, like with the dog, the food and the bell. The dog learned that the bell was associated with food and therefore started to salivate when the bell was heard. A new link was formed.

Skinner introduced the concept of operant conditioning. He showed this with pigeons who had a disc in their cage. If they pecked on this disc accidentally they got some food; gradually they realised the link between the disc and the reward (food) and so pecked all the time. Their new behaviour could be explained in terms of a reward or reinforcement. You also get negative reinforcement when an animal escapes from a negative stimulus. And punishment is the opposite of a reward and leads to a behaviour being stamped out.

The problem with these explanations is that they are good for animal behaviour but not as good for human behaviour because they do not take the mind into account. In an experiment with rats in a maze, it was shown that the rats did develop cognitive maps to help them solve the maze which means that the mind is part of learning even in animals.

The principles of conditioning have been used to explain how people learn abnormal behaviour. They might be rewarded for doing something strange and then continue to do this. Behavioural psychologists think you can use the same principles to teach people who are mentally ill to unlearn their abnormal behaviours and be taught new ones. Shaping can be used.

Gender behaviour can also be explained in terms of conditioning. Young boys and girls are rewarded with praise if they do things which are right for their gender and they may even be punished if they do things which are not gender-appropriate, so we can see that conditioning explains how they learn to behave. One problem with this account is that children also learn by imitating others. This is called social learning theory. If you imitate someone else then you must have a mental concept, and behaviourists only talk about the back box.

Another area of psychology is the acquisition of language. Skinner said that children learn language in the same way they learn everything else. They are rewarded when they say a word (they might get a biscuit) which encourages them to say it again. An adult may shape their behaviour so that if they say 'biccie' they are close to the word so they get a reward but the next time they have to get closer to get the reward. The alternative explanation was put forward by Chomsky

191

who said we acquire language because it is in our nature to do it. Obviously you learn words the way Skinner said, but grammar is acquired because it is innate. Studies have shown that parents do not reward speech consistently so it is hard to see how Skinner can be right.

Examiner's comment

This question calls for candidates both to outline some behaviourist theory and to apply it to a range of topics in psychology. The candidate has done this appropriately and has displayed a sound although fairly basic knowledge of both behavioural theory and the areas they have chosen to look at. This essay scored 11 marks out of a total of 24, which is generally equivalent to a weak grade D at A-level. Of the 12 marks available for skill A, it scored 6. Of the 12 available for skill B it scored 5. Throughout the essay the marks were limited by lack of depth and in some places clarity, particularly in respect of skill B.

In the second paragraph the candidate begins well by outlining the influence of behaviourist ideas throughout psychology, then attempts to describe Pavlov's study of classical conditioning of dogs but falls into the trap of assuming a detailed knowledge on the part of the reader. It is essential that when you describe a study you describe it *as if for someone who has no prior knowledge*.

In the third paragraph the candidate moves appropriately on to operant conditioning. Positive reinforcement is described reasonably well (although not named), but negative reinforcement and punishment, although clearly understood, are looked at in insufficient detail to gain much credit. The candidate does follow up with appropriate criticisms from a cognitive perspective, however, and gains skill B credit.

In the next paragraph the candidate applies behavioural principles to abnormal psychology. Although the principles are clearly put here, the use of an example of a particular disorder, and how this might be explained by maladaptive learning, would have made this section more meaningful. The idea of shaping has not been described clearly enough to gain credit. The next section of gender development is clearer but likewise would benefit from examples of what gender-appropriate behaviour might be reinforced and what might be punished. The candidate makes a good skill B point when introducing the importance of social learning in gender-acquisition.

The candidate concludes with a discussion of language acquisition. Skinner's approach is well described, but the candidate gets lost a bit and loses clarity in the discussion of the rival merits of Skinner's and Chomsky's approaches.

In conclusion this is a competent essay, well-focused on the question and showing good understanding. However, the marks are limited by depth of explanation and, occasionally, clarity of the answer.

KEY RESEARCH SUMMARY

A.R. Arthur (1998) Clinical psychologists, psychotherapists and orientation choice: does personality matter? *Proceedings of the British Psychological Society* **6 (2), 101.**

Introduction

In this book we have considered a wide range of theoretical approaches to psychology. As we established in Chapter 1 some psychologists are eclectic and draw on a range of approaches. Many psychologists, however, prefer to operate within one or perhaps two closely related paradigms such as behavioural and cognitive psychology. You will probably have found by this point that some approaches make much more sense to you than others. In Chapter 7 we looked at the possibility of social identity as a partial explanation of the way psychologists stick to their preferred theoretical approach. This recent study by Arthur is of interest to us because it suggests a second possible reason – that the personality and style of thinking of each psychologist affect what theoretical approach makes most sense to them. The study looks at therapists rather than psychologists in general, but is none the less revealing in showing that both personality and style of thinking differ considerably between professionals working with a psychodynamic approach and those working with cognitive and behavioural models.

Background

Past research has shown that psychologists, both academics and practitioners, have different theoretical preferences, and that these are at least partly a reflection of their personality and their style of thinking, more precisely of their epistemological style. Epistemology is the branch of philosophy that deals with the nature of knowledge. Epistemological style thus means the individual's approach to knowledge. It seems that not only do cognitive-behavioural and psychoanalytic therapists disagree on the aims and techniques of good therapy, but that they are completely unable to appreciate the other's perspective. In this study Arthur set out to examine the importance of both personality and epistemological style in affecting therapists' choice of theoretical orientation.

Method: 544 clinical psychologists and psychotherapists were invited to participate in the study. Of the 247 who agreed, 55 per cent were chartered clinical psychologists. The 113 psychoanalytic and 134 cognitive-behavioural therapists participating were sent three questionnaires by post. These were a personality test (called the MIPS) and two epistemological tests (called the OMPI and the PEP). They were also sent a further questionnaire in order to confirm that they actually practised and agreed with the theoretical model in which they were trained. The results were statistically analysed to reveal whether there was a difference between cognitive-behavioural and psychodynamic practitioners in personality or epistemological style.

Results: There were several significant differences in both personality and epistemological style between the psychodynamic and cognitive-behavioural practitioners. The psychoanalytic therapists were found to rely on intuition rather than physical senses to gather information. They were innovative in the way they organised information and preferred to look at the world as a whole rather than in parts. They were high in insight and empathy, and preferred to process information using metaphors and symbols, looking for qualitative rather than quantitative data. The cognitive-behavioural therapists preferred to use their senses rather than intuition to gather information and had a greater tendency to quantify information. The cognitive-behavioural group were found to be more conformist and conventional.

Discussion

This study shows, as we might expect, that psychodynamic and cognitive-behavioural practitioners differed significantly as people.

These results correspond closely to those of previous studies. Arthur has suggested that these characteristics are stable and therefore probably existed before their training – hence they were factors in choosing a theoretical orientation. It is of course also possible that the training of these professionals contributed to their epistemological style. This study therefore has the limitation that it is retrospective and assumes that the current measures of personality and epistemo-logical style were the same when the therapists chose a training.

Glossary

accommodation The formation of a new schema in order to accommodate a new piece of information.

actualisation The fulfilment of one's individual potential.

adaptive The quality of a behaviour or characteristic that aids the survival of the species because it renders it better adapted to its environment.

Alzheimer's disease A disease of the brain characterised by the loss of a large number of brain cells and resulting cognitive deficits.

animism A logical error typical of young children in which they attribute feelings and motives to inanimate objects.

anterograde amnesia A form of memory dysfunction in which the person becomes unable to store any new memories.

artificialism A logical error typical of young children in which natural phenomena are believed to be a result of human activity.

assimilation the process of incorporating new information into existing schemas.

attention deficit hyperactivity disorder (ADHD) A life-long condition that manifests in childhood. Symptoms include hyper-activity and difficulty in maintaining focused attention.

attribution The mental processes by which we make judgements about the reasons for people's actions, attributing these either to the nature of the person or to the situation.

average expectable environment From Scarr's theory, this is the typical range of quality of upbringing children are exposed to. Neglect and abuse fall outside the average expectable environment.

bodyclock A structure within the body which keeps time and maintains bodily rhythms.

castration anxiety In Freudian theory, the unconscious or pre-conscious belief that characterises boys during the Oedipus complex that their father will castrate them in response to their rivalry relationship.

child-centred An approach to teaching and learning that has as its central principle the idea that children learn best when carrying out tasks on their own or with help, as opposed to the more traditional 'chalk and talk' methods.

cognitive reductionism The tendency to explain psychological phenomena only by reference to cognitive processes and without taking into account other factors.

computer analogy A way of conceptualising human psychology that involves comparing the human mind to a computer.

computer simulation The use of computer software to generate a model of a cognitive process, in order to better understand how that process takes place in humans.

conditioned response The response to a conditioned stimulus.

conditioned stimulus A stimulus that has become associated with an unconditioned stimulus so that it elicits the same response as the unconditioned stimulus.

congruence In Rogerian theory, a close correspondence between the perceived self and the ideal self. In counselling, the quality of genuineness in the counsellor.

connectionist psychology A contemporary approach to cognitive psychology based on a modern understanding of the working of the human mind and the development of computers that function more like the human mind.

conservation The mental ability to realise that a given object remains the same despite changes in its appearance.

context-dependency The tendency to recall information better when in the same situation as when the information was learnt.

didactic An approach to teaching and learning in which the teacher directly instructs the learner, who in turn passively accepts the information.

discourse analysis The qualitative analysis of discourse, verbal, written or musical, in order to unpack hidden meanings and assumptions.

discrimination Treating people differently on the basis of one criterion such as gender or race.

disequilibrium The mental state in which one's existing schemas cannot explain a new piece of information.

dream-work The process by which latent content of a dream is transferred into manifest context.

ecological validity The quality in a psychological study of representing a real-life situation well. In practice this may mean conducting the study outside the laboratory – but not necessarily. What is important is that the study replicates the conditions of a real-life situation.

empathy The ability to sense and respond to the feelings of others.

equilibrium The mental state in which all information that is being perceived can be explained by existing schemas.

eugenics A political movement that advocates selective breeding of humans in order to improve the gene-pool.

evolution The tendency of a species to change its genetic make-up over many generations in order to aid its adaptation to its environment.

extinction A phenomenon of both classical and operant conditioning, whereby a learnt response or reinforced behaviour disappears over time.

false self In Winnicottian theory, the effect of the mother failing to cater for the emotional needs of the baby, leading to the child failing to develop a stable identity. The adult with a false self is characterised by a need to comply with the wishes of others.

fulfilment model The idea that counselling/therapy is not just to liberate people from past problems but also to help them fulfil their potential.

functional localisation The tendency for different parts of the brain to take on specific roles.

gender schema A mental structure containing all of our knowledge, beliefs and feelings about gender, including our own gender identity.

generalisation A phenomenon of classical conditioning whereby a conditioned response becomes generalised to stimuli similar in some way to the conditioned stimulus.

genetics The study of inheritance.

genocide Mass extermination with the intention to eliminate a group completely.

good enough mother From Winnicottian theory, the idea of the mother who successfully adjusts to coping with the emotional needs of the baby and caters sufficiently to its needs.

heritability The extent to which an individual characteristic is acquired by the passing on of genes from parents as opposed to being acquired as a result of environmental influences.

hippocampus A structure within the temporal lobe of the brain that is believed to be important in the process of storing new memories.

homophobia A negative response to lesbians and gay men, characterised by fear, hatred or anger.

mental discovery The mental process by which we derive new knowledge by making connections between pieces of existing knowledge.

metacognitive skills Skills in understanding one's own mental processes.

moral realism A type of moral reasoning in which someone (usually a child) is able only to appreciate the moral implications of a situation from one person's point of view.

negative punishment A response to a behaviour that involves the removal of a pleasurable stimulus in order to reduce the probability of that behaviour being repeated.

negative reinforcement A response to a behaviour that involves the removal of an unpleasant stimulus and increases the probability of that behaviour being repeated.

neurophysiology The study of the nervous system.

neutral operant A response to a behaviour that neither increases nor decreases the probability of the behaviour being repeated.

neutral stimulus A stimulus that does not elicit a response.

object relations school (of psychodynamic psychology) A British post-Freudian school including famous names such as Fairbairn, Winnicott and Guntrip. Characterised by an emphasis on the importance of children's instinct to form relationships and the importance of these early relationships in later life.

Oedipus complex The three-way family dynamic in which a rivalry develops between a child and one parent for the attention and affection of the other parent. In Freudian theory this is an important developmental stage, taking place between 3 and 6 years of age.

operant A response to a behaviour that has an impact on whether that behaviour becomes reinforced or not.

operant behaviour Behaviour that has been learnt in response to operants.

operations Our mental representations of the rules by which the world works.

organ-pleasure In Freudian theory, the focusing of libido on particular organs at different ages.

paradigm An overarching approach to psychology, including a set of theories and favoured research methods.

peak experience In Maslow's theory, moments when the world feels complete and one feels at one with the world.

penis envy In Freudian theory the idea that girls in Oedipal conflict believe on an unconscious or preconscious level that they have already been castrated by their rivalrous mother.

person-centred counselling A non-directive style of counselling based on the work of Rogers. Emphasises the importance of empathy, genuineness and unconditional positive regard on the part of the counsellor.

positive discipline An approach to disciplining children that emphasises positive reinforcement for appropriate behaviour and minimises the use of punishment.

positive punishment A response to a behaviour that introduces an unpleasant stimulus in order to reduce the probability of the behaviour being repeated.

positive reinforcement A response to a behaviour that involves a reward and increases the probability of that behaviour being repeated.

psychoanalysis A type of psychodynamic therapy characterised by very long-term and intensive treatment and strict adherence to psychodynamic techniques. Also used as an alternative term for psychodynamic psychology – generally preferred by those who see this field as outside mainstream psychology.

psychodynamic psychology An approach to psychology emphasising the importance of early relationships and trauma, and the influence of unconscious mental processes on behaviour.

psychological social psychology The tradition of social psychology that emphasises experimental research.

radical behaviourism An approach to psychology that explains all behaviour in terms of operant conditioning.

recovered memory A memory that has been forgotten and is later remembered, often (though not necessarily) in therapy.

reductionism The tendency to explain complex psychological phenomena by reference to only one factor, such as learning or biology.

reinforcers Responses to a behaviour that increase the probability of that behaviour being repeated.

respondent behaviour Behaviour that depends on reflexes and does not require learning.

retrospective studies Studies that involve participants remembering events that have happened in the past.

rhythms Cycles of bodily activity.

scaffolding The processes by which teachers guide learners through tasks.

schemas Units of memory, each of which represents all our information on one aspect of the world.

self-esteem Our feelings towards ourselves (i.e. we like ourselves).

social cognition The mental processes that we use in social situations, including attribution and stereotyping.

social comparison The process of comparing ourselves, and any group with which we might identify ourselves, with others.

social constructionism An approach to psychology that emphasises the social construction of knowledge and political and historical factors that have influenced the development of psychological concepts and theories.

social identification The adoption of the identity of a group.

sociological social psychology The tradition of social psychology that emphasises political issues.

spirituality An aspect of human experience characterised by one's relationship with the universe.

state-dependency The tendency to recall information better when in the same physiological state as when the information was learnt.

structural model Freud's later model of the mind consisting of 'I', 'it' and 'above-I'.

token economy Tokens are given in response to appropriate behaviour. These can then be exchanged for a further reward in order to reinforce the behaviour.

topographical model Freud's model of the mind consisting of the conscious, preconscious and unconscious minds.

transpersonal psychology An approach to psychology that emphasises the role of spirituality.

unconditional positive regard Acceptance from others that is not dependent on complying to their wishes.

unconditioned response An innate response to an unconditioned stimulus.

unconditioned stimulus A stimulus that elicits a response without a process of conditioning.

uncontrollable reinforcers Apparent responses to a behaviour that increase the probability of that behaviour being repeated, but which are not in fact contingent on that behaviour.

valuing process In Rogerian theory, an unconscious tendency to choose behaviours that will help us to achieve our potential.

vicarious reinforcement Witnessed responses to a behaviour in others that result in an increased probability that the behaviour will be imitated or repeated by the observer.

zeitgebers Literal translation 'time-keepers'. Environmental cues that reset the body clock or clocks.

References

Adams, H., Wright, L. and Lohr, B. (1996) Is homophobia associated with homosexual arousal? *Journal of Abnormal Psychology* 105 (3), 440–445.

Aggleton, J.P. and Waskett, L. (1999) The ability of odours to serve as state-dependent cues for real-world memories. Can Viking smells aid the recall of Viking experiences? *British Journal of Psychology* 90 (1), 1–18.

Akerstedt, T. (1985) Adjustment of physiological circadian rhythms and the sleep–wake cycle to shiftwork. In S. Folkard and T.H. Monk, *Hours of work*. Chichester, John Wiley & Sons.

Archer, J. (1996) Evolutionary social psychology. In M. Hewstone, W. Stroebe and G.M. Stephenson, *Introduction to social psychology*. Oxford, Blackwell.

Atkinson, R.C. and Shiffrin, R.M. (1968) Human memory: a proposal system and its control processes. In K.W. Spence and J. Spence (eds) *The Psychology of Learning and Motivation, Vol. 2*. Academic Press.

Atkinson, R.L., Atkinson, R.C., Smith, E.E. and Bem, D.K. (1993) *Introduction to psychology*. London, Harcourt Brace Jovanovich.

Baddeley, A.D. (1986) *Working memory*. Oxford, Oxford University Press.

Baddeley, A.D. (1990) *Human memory*. Hove, Lawrence Erlbaum Associates.

Baddeley, A.D. (1994) *Your memory: a user's guide*. London, Penguin.

Baddeley, A.D., Thomson, N. and Buchanan, D. (1975) Word length and the structure of short term memory. *Journal of Verbal Learning and Verbal Behaviour* 14, 575–589.

Bailey, M. (1993) Science and the fear of knowledge. *Chicago Tribune* (opinions page).

Baillargeon, R. and DeVos, J. (1991) Object permanence in young infants: further evidence. *Child Development* 62, 1227–1246.

Bandura, A. (1978) *Social learning theory*. Englewood Cliffs, Prentice-Hall.

Bandura, A., Ross, D. and Ross, S.A. (1961) Transmission of aggression through imitation of aggressive models. *Journal of Abnormal and Social Psychology* 63 (3), 575–582.

Banyard, P. (1999) *Controversies in psychology*. London, Routledge.

Baron, R.A. and Byrne, D. (1994) *Social psychology: understanding human interaction*. Boston, Allyn and Bacon.

Bateman, A. and Holmes, J. (1995) *Introduction to psychoanalysis*. London, Routledge.

Beattie, G. and Coughlan, J. (1999) An experimental investigation of the role of iconic gestures in lexical access using the tip of the tongue phenomenon. *British Journal of Psychology* 90 (1), 35–56.

Beaumont, J.G. (1988) *Understanding neuropsychology*. Oxford, Blackwell.

Beck, A.T. (1979) *Cognitive therapy and the emotional disorders*. New York, Basic Books.

Bennet, N. and Dunn, E. (1992) *Managing classroom groups*. Hemel Hempstead, Simon & Schuster.

Bentley, A. (1994) Counselling and homelessness. *Counselling* 5 (2), 132–134.

Bentley, E. (1999) *Awareness: biorhythms, sleep and dreaming*. London, Routledge.

Bettelheim, B. (1985) *Freud and man's soul*. London, Flamingo.

Bifulco, A., Brown, G.W. and Alder, Z. (1991) Early sexual abuse and clinical depression in later life. *British Journal of Psychiatry* 159, 115–122.

Black, S.L. and Bevan, S. (1992) At the movies with Buss and Durkee: a natural experiment on film violence. *Aggressive Behaviour* 18, 37–45.

Blass, T. (1993) *What we now know about obedience: distillations from 30 years of research on the Milgram paradigm.* Annual meeting of the APA, Toronto.

Bowlby, J. (1969) *Attachment & loss.* London, Pimlico.

Bradmetz, J. (1999) Precursors of formal thought: a longitudinal study. *British Journal of Developmental Psychology* 17, 61–81.

Briere, J. and Conte, J.R. (1993) Self-reported amnesia for abuse in adults molested as children. *Journal of Traumatic Stress* 6, 21–31.

Brown, D. and Pedder, J. (1991) *Introduction to psychotherapy.* London, Routledge.

Bruce, V. (1982) Changing faces: visual and non-visual coding processes in face recognition. *British Journal of Psychology* 73, 105–116.

Burns, A. (1998) Pop psychology or Ken behaving badly. *The Psychologist* 11 (7), 360.

Burr, V. (1995) *Introduction to social constructionism.* London, Routledge.

Burr, V. (1998) Overview: realism, relativism, social constructionism and discourse. In I. Parker, *Social constructionism, discourse and reality.* London, Sage.

Burton, M. and Davey, T. (1996) The psychodynamic paradigm. In R. Woolfe and W. Dryden (eds) *Handbook of counselling psychology.* London, Sage.

Bushman, B.J. (1988) The effects of apparel on compliance: a field experiment with a female authority figure. *Personality and Social Psychology Bulletin* 14, 459–467.

Buss, D.M. (1995) Evolutionary psychology: a new paradigm for psychological science. *Psychological Inquiry* 6, 1–30.

Buss, D.M. and Schmidt, D.P. (1993) Sexual strategies theory: an evolutionary perspective of human mating. *Psychological Review* 100, 204–232.

Carlson, N. (1998) *The physiology of behaviour.* Boston, Allyn & Bacon

Cave, S. (1999) *Therapeutic approaches in psychology.* London, Routledge.

Ceci, S.J. (1994) Cognitive and social factors in children's testimony. In B. Sales and G. Vandenbos (eds) *Psychology in litigation and legislation.* Washington, DC, American Psychological Association.

Ceci, S.J. and Bruck, M. (1993) Suggestibility of the child witness: a historical review and synthesis. *Psychological Bulletin* 113, 403–439.

Chorney, M.J., Seese, K., Owen, M.J., Daniels, J., McGuffin, P., Thompson, L.A., Detterman, D.K., Benbow, C.P., Lubinsky, D., Eley, T.C. and Plomin, R. (1998) A quantitative trait locus (QTL) associated with cognitive ability in children. *Psychological Science* 9, 159–166.

Christo, G. (1997) Child sexual abuse: psychological consequences. *The Psychologist* 10 (5), 205–209.

Clamp, A. and Russell, J. (1998) *Comparative psychology*. London, Hodder & Stoughton.

Cohen, G., Kiss, G. and le Voi, M. (1993) *Memory: current issues*, 2nd edition. Milton Keynes, Open University Press.

Collins, A.M. and Quillian, M.R. (1969) Retrieval time from semantic memory. *Journal of Verbal Learning and Verbal Behaviour* 8, 240–248.

Condor, S. (1988) 'Race stereotypes' and racist discourse. *Text* 8, 69–91.

Coopersmith, S. (1967) *The antecedents of self-esteem*. San Francisco, Freeman.

Crook, C. (1994) *Computers and the collaborative experience of learning*. London, Routledge.

Dare, C. (1997) Psychotherapy B: analytically informed. In R. Murray, P. Hill and P. McGuffin (eds) *The essentials of postgraduate psychiatry*. Cambridge, Cambridge University Press.

Darwin, C. (1859) *The origin of species*. London, John Murray.

Darwin, C. (1871) *The descent of man, and selection in relation to sex*. London, John Murray.

Dement, W. and Kleitman, N. (1957) The relation of eye movements during sleep to dream activity: an objective method for the study of dreaming. *Journal of Experimental Psychology* 53 (5), 339–346.

Dement, W.C. and Wolpert, E. (1958) The relation of eye movements, bodily movements and external stimuli to dream content. *Journal of Experimental Psychology* 55, 543–553.

Doherty, K. and Anderson, I. (1998) Perpetuating rape-supportive culture: talking about rape. *The Psychologist* 11 (12), 583–587.

Dollard, J. and Miller, N.E. (1950) *Personality and psychotherapy:*

an analysis in terms of learning, thinking and culture. New York, McGraw-Hill.

Ebstein, R.P. and Belmaker, R.H. (1997) Saga of an adventure gene: novelty seeking, substance abuse and dopamine D4 receptor exon III polymorphism. *Molecular Psychiatry* 2, 381–384.

Ebstein, R.P., Novick, O., Umansky, R., Priel, B., Osher, Y. and Blaine, D. (1995) Dopamine receptor D4exon III polymorphism associated with the human personality trait of novelty seeking. *Nature Genetics* 12, 78–80.

Eden, G.F., VanMeter, J.W., Rumsey, J.M., Maisog, J., Woods, R.P. and Zeffiro, T.A. (1996) Abnormal processing of visual motion in dyslexia revealed by functional brain imaging. *Nature* 382, 66–69.

Engler, B. (1999) *Personality theories: an introduction*. Boston, Houghton-Mifflin.

Eysenck, M. (1998) Memory. In M. Eysenck (ed.) *Psychology: an integrated approach*. Harlow, Addison-Wesley Longman.

Faulkner, D. (1995) Teaching and learning. In D. Bancroft and R. Carr (eds) *Influencing children's development*. Milton Keynes, Open University.

Flanagan, C. (1999) *Early socialisation: sociability and attachment*. London, Routledge.

Flin, R., Boon, J., Knox, A. and Bull, R. (1992) The effect of a five month delay on children's and adults' eyewitness testimony. *British Journal of Psychology* 83, 323–336.

Folkard, S. (1996) Bags of time to play. *Daily Express*, 28 September.

Foot, H., Morgan, M. and Shute, R. (1990) *Children helping children*. Chichester, John Wiley & Sons.

Freud, S. (1900) *The interpretation of dreams*. London, Hogarth Press.

Freud, S. (1905) Three essays on sexuality. London, Hogarth Press.

Freud, S. (1909) Analysis of a phobia in a 9-year old boy. *Collected papers* vol. III, 149–295.

Freud, S. (1917) *Introductory lectures on psychoanalysis*. London, Hogarth Press.

Freud, S. (1920) *A general introduction to psychoanalysis*. New York, Washington Square Press.

Freud, S. (1924) *The dissolution of the Oedipus complex*. Standard Edition vol. 19. London, Hogarth Press.

Freud, S. (1933) *New introductory lectures on psychoanalysis*. London, Hogarth Press.

Gaertner, S.L., Mann, J.A., Murrell, A.J. and Dovidio, J.F. (1989) Reducing intergroup bias: the benefits of recategorisation. *Journal of Personality and Social Psychology* 57, 239–249.

Gaertner, S.L., Mann, J.A., Dovidio, J.F., Murrell, A.J. and Pomare, M. (1990) How does cooperation reduce intergroup bias? *Journal of Personality and Social Psychology* 59, 692–704.

Gaertner, S.L., Rust, M.C., Divisio, J.C., Bachman, B.A. and Anastasio, P. (1993) The contact hypothesis: the role of a common in-group identity on reducing intergroup bias. *Small Business Research*.

Gevins, A.S., Leong, J., Smith, M.E., Le, J. and Du, R. (1995) Mapping cognitive brain function with modern high-resolution encephalography. *Trends in the Neurosciences* 18, 429–436.

Gilbert, D.T., Pelham, B.W. and Krull, D.S. (1988) On cognitive business: when person perceivers meet persons perceived. *Journal of Personality and Social Psychology* 54, 733–740.

Glick, P. and Fiske, S.T. (1996) The ambivalent sexism inventory: differentiating hostile and benevolent sexism. *Journal of Personality and Social Psychology* 70, 491–512.

Godden, D.R. and Baddeley, A.D. (1975) Context-dependent memory in two natural environments: on land and under water. *British Journal of Psychology* 66, 325–331.

Goren, C.C., Sarty, M. and Wu, R.W.K. (1975) Visual following and pattern discrimination of face-like stimuli by new-born infants. *Paediatrics* 56, 544–549.

Greenberg, L.S., Elliott, R.K. and Liaeter, G. (1994) Research on experiential therapies. In A.E. Bergin and S.L. Garfield (eds) *Handbook of psychotherapy and behaviour change*. New York, John Wiley & Sons.

Groome, D., Dewart, H., Esgate, A., Gurney, K., Kemp, R. and Towell, N. (1999) *Cognitive psychology, processes and disorders*. Hove, Psychology Press.

Gross, R. (1996) *Psychology, the science of mind and behaviour*. London, Hodder & Stoughton.

Grunbaum, A. (1993) *Validation in the clinical theory of psychoanalysis*. New York, International Universities Press.

Hardman, D. (1999) Qualitative vs quantitative again. *The Psychologist* 12 (2), 65–66.

Harkness, M. (1998) The story of Percy the propositions prototype (or the Mini with motivation). *Person-centred Practice* 6 (2), 104–109.

Harris, K. and Campbell, E.A. (1999) The plans in unplanned pregnancy: secondary gain and the partnership. *British Journal of Medical Psychology* 72 (1), 105–120.

Hatcher, D. (1997) Male and female worlds: students' views of domestic tasks. *Psychology Teaching* 5, 46–98.

Haxby, J.V., Grady, C.L., Horwitz, B., Ungerleider, L.G., Mishkin, M., Carson, R.E., Schapiro, M.B. and Rapoport, S.I. (1991) Functional associations among human posterior extrastiate brain regions during object and spatial vision. *Proceedings of the National Academy of Sciences USA* 88, 1621–1625,

Hayes, N. (1998) *Foundations of psychology* (2nd edn). Walton-on-Thames, Nelson.

Henderson, J. (1999) *Memory and forgetting*. London, Routledge.

Hetherington, A.W. and Ranson, S.W. (1942) The relation of various hypothalamic lesions to adiposity in the rat. *Journal of Comparative Neurology* 76, 475–499.

Hill, H. and Bruce, V. (1996) Effects of lighting on the perception of facial surfaces. *Journal of Experimental Psychology: Human Perception and Performance* 22, 986–1004.

Hobson, J.A. (1988) *The dreaming brain*. New York, Basic Books.

Hobson, J.A. (1989) *Sleep*. New York, Scientific American Library.

Hobson, J.A. and McCarley, R.W. (1977) The brain as a dream-state generator: an activation–synthesis hypothesis of the dream process. *American Journal of Psychiatry* 134, 1335–1348.

Horowitz, M., Rosenberg, S.M., and Bartholomew, K. (1993) Interpersonal problems, attachment styles and outcome in brief psychodynamic therapy. *Journal of Consulting and Clinical Psychology* 61 (4), 549–560.

Howe, M.J.A. (1997) *IQ in question: the truth about intelligence*. London, Sage.

Hunter, C.E. and Ross, M.W. (1991) Determinants of health-care workers' attitudes towards people with AIDS. *Journal of Applied Social Psychology* 21, 947–956.

Inhelder, B. and Piaget, J. (1958) *The growth of logical thinking from childhood to adolescence*. London, Routledge & Kegan Paul.

Jacobs, M. (1992) *Sigmund Freud*. London, Sage.

Jacobs, M. (1995) *D.W. Winnicott*. London, Sage.

Jarvis, M. (1998) Integrating traditional theories of attribution with contemporary theory and application. *Psychology Teaching* 6, 4–20.

Jarvis, M. (2000) Teaching psychodynamic psychology: from discourse analysis towards a model of reflective practice. *Psychology Teaching*.

Jerabek, I. and Standing, L. (1992) Imagined test situations produce contextual memory enhancement. *Perceptual and Motor Skills* 75, 400.

Johnston, M. (1997) *Developmental cognitive neuroscience*. Oxford, Blackwell.

Jones, E. (1951) *The life and works of Sigmund Freud*. New York, Basic Books.

Jung, C.G. (1923) *Psychological types*. New York, Harcourt Brace & Co.

Keckland, G. and Akerstadt, T. (1993) Sleepiness in long distance truck drivers: an ambulatory EEG study of night driving. *Ergonomics* 36 (9), 1007–1017.

Kessler, R.C. and Magee, W.J. (1993) Childhood adversities and adult depression: basic patterns of association in a US national survey. *Psychological Medicine* 23, 679–690.

Kimura, D. (1996) Sex, sexual orientation and sex hormones influence human cognitive function. *Current Opinion in Neurobiology* 6, 259–263.

Kitayama, S. and Markus, H.R. (1992) *Construal of self as cultured frame: implications for internationalising psychology*. Symposium on Internationalism and Higher Education. Ann Arbor, MI.

Kitzinger, C., Coyle, A., Wilkinson, S. and Wilson, M. (1998) Towards lesbian and gay psychology. *The Psychologist* 11 (11), 529–534.

Knight, B. and Johnston, A. (1997) The role of movement in face-recognition. *Visual Cognition* 4, 265–273.

Kohn, A. (1993) *Punished by rewards*. Boston, Houghton-Mifflin.

Kramarski, B. and Mevarech, Z.R. (1997) Cognitive–metacognitive training within a problem-solving based Logo environment. *British Journal of Educational Psychology* 67 (4), 425–446.

Lacan, J. (1966) Function et champ de la parole et du langage en psychoanalyse. *Ecrits*. Paris, Seuil.

LaHoste, G.J., Swanson, J.M., Wigal, S.S., Glabe, C., Wigal, T. and King, N. (1996) Dopamine D4 receptor gene polymorphism is associated with attention deficit hyperactivity disorder. *Molecular Psychiatry* 1, 128–131.

LeDoux, J.E. (1993) Emotional networks in the brain. In M. Lewis and J.M. Haviland (eds) *Handbook of Emotions.* New York, Guilford Press.

Lemma-Wright, A. (1995) *Invitation to psychodynamic psychology.* London, Whurr.

Lerman, H. (1992) The limits of phenomenology: a feminist critique of the humanistic personality theories. in L.S. Brown and M. Ballou (eds) *Personality and Psychopathology.* New York, Guildford Press.

Littleton, K. (1995) Children and computers. In D. Bancroft and R. Carr, *Influencing children's development.* Milton Keynes, Open University.

Loftus, E.F. (1975) Leading questions and the eyewitness report. *Cognitive Psychology* 7, 560–572.

Loftus, E.F. (1995) Memories of childhood trauma or trauma of childhood memories. Paper presented at the annual conference of the American Psychological Association, New York.

Loftus, E.F. and Zanni, G. (1975) Eyewitness testimony: the influence of the wording of a question. *Bulletin of the Psychonomic Society* 5, 86–88.

Logie, R.H. (1986) Visuospatial processes in working memory. *Quarterly Journal of Experimental Psychology* 38A, 229–247.

Logie, R.H. (1999) Working memory. *The Psychologist* 12 (4), 174–178.

Lundin, R.W. (1996) *Theories and systems of psychology.* Lexington, Heath.

McGarrigle, J. and Donaldson, M. (1974) Conservation accidents. *Cognition* 3, 341–350.

McGhee, P. (1998) Experimental social psychology. In R. Sapsford, A. Still, M. Wetherall, D. Miell and R. Stevens (eds) *Theory and social psychology.* London, Sage.

Marshall, W.L. and Barbaree, H.E. (1988) The long-term evaluation of a behavioural treatment programme for child molesters. *Behaviour Research and Therapy* 26, 499–511.

Martin, C.L. and Halverson, C.F. (1981) A schematic processing model of sex-typing and stereotyping in children. *Child Development* 52, 1119–1134.

Maslow, A. (1954) *Motivation and personality*, 1st edition. New York, Harper & Row.

Maslow, A. (1970) *Motivation and personality*, 2nd edition. New York, Harper & Row.

Matute, H. (1996) Illusion of control: detecting response-outcome in analytic but not in realistic conditions. *Psychological Science* 7, 289–293.

Matute, H. (1998) The learning perspective. In M. Eysenck (ed.) *Psychology: an integrated approach.* Harlow, Addison-Wesley Longman.

Maurice, D. (1998) The Von Sallmann lecture 1996: an ophthalmological explanation of REM sleep. *Experimental Eye Research* 66 (2), 139–145.

Mayhew, J. (1997) *Psychological change, a practical introduction.* Basingstoke, Macmillan.

Mearns, D. and Thorne, B. (1988) *Person-centred counselling in action.* London, Sage.

Meddis, R. (1975) On the function of sleep. *Animal Behaviour* 23, 676–691.

Merry, T. (1995) *Invitation to person-centred psychology.* London, Whurr.

Merry, T. (1998) Editorial. *Person-centred Practice* 6 (2), 66–67.

Mevarech, Z., Silber, O. and Fine, D. (1991) Learning with computers in small groups: cognitive and affective outcomes. *Journal of Educational Computing Research* 7 (2), 233–243.

Milgram, S. (1963) Behavioural study of obedience. *Journal of Abnormal and Social Psychology* 67, 371–378.

Milgram, S. (1974) *Obedience to authority.* New York, Harper & Row.

Minsky, R. (1998) *Psychoanalysis and culture.* Cambridge, Polity Press.

Morgan, E. (1995) Measuring time with a biological clock. *Biological Sciences Review* 7, 2–5.

Myers, L.B. and Brewin, C.R. (1994) Recall of early experiences and the repressive coping style. *Journal of Abnormal Psychology* 103, 288–292.

Needleman, H.L., Schell, A., Bellinger, D. and Leviton, A. (1996) Bone lead levels and delinquent behaviour. *Journal of the American Medical Association* 275, 363–369.

Newman, H.H., Freeman, F.N. and Holzinger, K.J. (1937) *Twins: a study of heredity and environment*. Chicago, University of Chicago Press.

Novak, R.D., Smolensky, M.H., Fairchild, E.J. and Reeves, R.R. (1990) Shiftwork and industrial injuries at a chemical plant in South East Texas. *Chronobiology International* 7, 155–164.

Owusu-Bempah, K. and Howitt, D. (1994) Racism and the psychology textbook. *The Psychologist* 7 (4), 163–166.

Oswald, I. (1976) The function of sleep. *Postgraduate Medical Journal* 52 (603) 15–18.

Papert, S. (1980) *Mindstorms: children, computers and powerful ideas*. Brighton, Harvester Press.

Pavlov, I.P. ([1856] 1927) *The conditioned reflex*. London, Oxford University Press.

Phillips, J.L. (1975) *The origins of intellect: Piaget's theory*. San Francisco, Freeman.

Piaget, J. (1952) *Logic and psychology*. Series of lectures at Manchester University. New York, Basic Books 1957.

Piaget, J. (1963) *The origins of intelligence in children*. New York, Norton.

Piaget, J. (1972) Intellectual evolution from adolescence to adulthood. *Human Development* 15, 1–12.

Piaget, J. and Inhelder, B. (1956) *The child's conception of space*. London, Routledge & Kegan Paul.

Plomin, R. (1988) The nature and nurture of cognitive abilities. In R. Sternberg (ed.) *Advances in the psychology of human intelligence* 4. Hillsdale, Erlbaum.

Plomin, R., DeFries, J.C., McClearn, G.E. and Rutter, M. (1997) *Behavioural genetics*. New York, Freeman.

Richardson, K. (1997) Letter to *The Psychologist* 19 (2).

Rogers, C. (1959) A theory of therapy, personality and interpersonal relationships, as developed in the client-centred framework. In S. Koch (ed.) *Psychology: a study of a science* vol. 3. New York, McGraw-Hill.

Rogers, C. (1961) *On becoming a person: a therapist's view of psychotherapy*. Boston, Houghton-Mifflin.

Rowan, J. (1990) *Transpersonal psychology*. London, Routledge.

Rowan, J. (1998) Qualitative vs quantitative. *The Psychologist* 11 (12), 578.

Rycroft, C. (1968) *A critical dictionary of psychoanalysis*. London, Penguin.

Scarr, S. (1992) Developmental theories for the 1990s: development and individual differences. *Child Development* 63, 1–19.

Schwartz, W., Recht, L. and Lew, R. (1995) Three time zones and you're out. *New Scientist* 29, October.

Searle, A. (1999) *Introducing research and data in psychology: a guide to methods and analysis*. London, Routledge.

Shaywitz, B.A., Shaywitz, S.E., Pugh, K.R., Constable, R.T., Skudlarski, P., Fulbright, R.K., Bronen, R.A., Fletcher, J.M., Shankweiler, D.P., Katz, L. and Gore, J.C. (1995) Sex differences in the functional organisation of the brain for language. *Nature* 373, 607–609.

Shields, J. (1962) *Monozygotic twins brought up apart and brought up together*. London, Oxford University Press.

Silber, K. (1999) *The physiological basis of behaviour: neural and hormonal processes*. London, Routledge.

Silverman, I. and Eals, M. (1992) Sex differences in spatial abilities: evolutionary theory and data. In J.H. Barlow, L. Cosmides and J. Tooby (eds) *The adapted mind*. New York, Oxford University Press,

Skal, D. (1993) *The monster show: a cultural history of horror*. London, Plexus.

Skellington, D. (1995) *Psychology and race*. London, Sage.

Skinner, B.F. (1938) *The behaviour of organisms: an experimental analysis*. New York, Appleton-Century-Croft.

Skinner, B.F. (1948) Superstition in the pigeon. *Journal of experimental psychology* 38, 168–172.

Skinner, B.F. (1974) *About behaviourism*. London, Jonathan Cape.

Skinner, L., Berry, K. and Griffith, S. (1995) Generalisability and specificity of the stigma associated with the mental illness label: a reconsideration 25 years later. *Journal of Community Psychology* 23.

Smith, P.K., Cowie, H. and Blades, M. (1998) *Understanding children's development*. London, Blackwell

Solms, M. (1995) New findings on the neurological organisation of dreaming: implications for psychoanalysis. *Psychoanalytic Quarterly* 64 (1), 43–67.

Springer, S.P. and Deutsch, G. (1998) *Left brain right brain: perspectives from cognitive neuroscience*. New York, Freeman.

Stewart, J. and Amir, S. (1998) Body clocks get tired and emotional. *New Scientist* 21 (November).

Still, A. (1998) Historical roots of social psychology. In R. Sapsford, A. Still, M. Wetherall, D. Miell and R. Stevens (eds) *Theory and Social Psychology*. Milton Keynes, Open University Press.

Stirling, J. (1999) *Cortical functions*. London, Routledge.

Tajfel, H. and Turner, J.C. (1979) An integrative theory of intergroup conflict. In W.G. Austin and S. Worchel (eds) *The social psychology of intergroup relations*. Cambridge, Cambridge University Press.

Tavris, C. and Wade, C. (1997) *Psychology in perspective*. New York, Longman.

Thorndike, E.L. (1898) Animal intelligence: an experimental study of the associative processes in animals. *Psychological Review Monograph Supplement* 2 (whole no. 8).

Thorne, B. (1992) *Carl Rogers*. London, Sage.

Thorne, B. (1993) Spirituality and the counsellor. In W. Dryden (ed.) *Questions and answers on counselling in action*. London, Sage.

Trevarthen, C. (1995) The child's need to learn a culture. *Children and Society* 9 (1), 5–19.

Tulving, E. (1972) Episodic and semantic memory. In E. Tulving and W. Donaldson (eds) *Organisation of memory*. London, Academic Press.

Tulving, E. (1987) Multiple memory systems and consciousness. *Human Neurobiology* 6, 67–80.

Tulving, E. (1989) Memory: performance, knowledge and experience. *European Journal of Cognitive Psychology* 1, 3–26.

Watson, J.B. (1913) Psychology as the behaviourist views it. *Psychological Review* 20, 158–177.

Watson, J.B. (1919) *Psychology from the standpoint of a behaviourist*. Philadelphia, Lippincott.

Watson, J.B. (1925) *Behaviourism*. New York, W.W. Norton.

Watson, J.B. and Rayner, R. (1920) Conditioned emotional responses. *Journal of Experimental Psychology* 3, 1–14.

Watson, S.J. and Akil, H. (1999) Gene chips and arrays revealed: a primer on their power and uses. *Biological Psychiatry* 45, 533–543.

Wetherall, M. (1997) *Identities, groups and social issues*. London, Sage.

Winnicott, D.W. (1958) *The maturational process and the facilitating environment*. London, Maresfield Library.

Winnicott, D.W. (1965) *The family and individual development*. London, Tavistock Publications.

Winnicott, D.W. (1988) *Babies and their mothers*. London, Free Association Books.

Wood, D.J., Bruner, J.S. and Ross, G. (1976) The role of tutoring in problem-solving. *Journal of Child Psychology and Psychiatry* 17, 89–100.

Yuille, J.C. and Cutshall, J.L. (1986) A case-study of eye-witness memory of a crime. *Journal of Applied Psychology* 71, 291–301.

Index

Index complied by Emma Chandler